Contents

Foreword

We become what we behold. And when, in faith and through prayer, we willingly receive and accept how Jesus beholds us, a light penetrates our hearts. This light is the active presence of the Holy Spirit. In a real sense, the laboring love of the Holy Spirit heals us from seeing ourselves through the demeaning lies of this world and through the accusatory tactics of the evil one. Instead, the light of the Holy Spirit strengthens us to see ourselves as the radiant beauty that we are, as beloved sons and daughters of the Father in and through Jesus (Matthew 3:17).

To see ourselves in the light of the Holy Spirit is to see ourselves through Jesus' eyes. It is a light that cannot be overcome by any darkness (John 1:5). St. Clare's instructions to her sisters encourages all of us: "For his is the splendor of eternal glory, the brightness of eternal light, and the mirror without cloud. Queen and bride of Jesus Christ, look into that mirror daily and study well your reflection, that you may adorn yourself, mind and body."[1]

As Christian disciples on mission, we need to learn how to identify and surrender to the light of the Holy Spirit so that we can enjoy, in friendship with Jesus, the spiritual inheritance that he has gained for us. The more we learn to live in this friendship and receive the Holy Spirit, the more we will attract others through a contagion of hope. This is the hope that evangelizes the world! We live each day in a manner that gives witness to this hope, which is born of friendship with Jesus. Surely it

HOW TO
WIN FRIENDS
FOR CHRIST

ONE CONVERSATION

AT A TIME

HOW TO
WIN FRIENDS
FOR CHRIST

ONE CONVERSATION

AT A TIME

Fr. Thomas Cavanaugh and John D. Love

the WORD among us® press

Published by The Word Among Us Press
7115 Guilford Drive
Frederick, Maryland 21704

21 20 19 18 17   1 2 3 4 5

ISBN: 978-1-59325-308-0
eISBN: 978-1-59325-492-6

Nihil Obstat: Rev. Paul F. deLadurantaye, S.T.D.
　Censor Librorum

Imprimatur: +Paul S. Loverde, Bishop of Arlington
　February 4, 2016

The *Nihil Obstat* and *Imprimatur* are official declarations that a book or pamphlet is free of doctrinal or moral error. No implication is contained herein that those who have granted the *Nihil Obstat* or *Imprimatur* agree with the contents, opinions, or statements expressed.

Scripture texts in this work are taken from the *New American Bible, Revised Edition* © 2010, 1991, 1986, 1970 Confraternity of Christian Doctrine, Washington, D.C. and are used by permission of the copyright owner. All rights reserved. No part of the *New American Bible* may be reproduced in any form without permission in writing from the copyright owner.

Cover design by David Crosson

Made and printed in the United States of America

Library of Congress Control Number: 2017934028

pleases the Father to give us the kingdom, to have us taste and see God's reign in everyday faith (Luke 12:32). He is pouring the Holy Spirit into our hearts at this present moment (Romans 5:5). We are being beheld by Love!

Several years ago, Fr. Thomas Cavanaugh made a thirty-day silent retreat, the Spiritual Exercises of St. Ignatius of Loyola, and entered into an intense intimate encounter with the indwelling Trinity. In the light of the Holy Spirit, he was given a new depth of passionate friendship with Jesus as well as a call to evangelize hearts by inviting others into the warmth and beauty of this friendship.

Fr. Thomas returned to the seminary, and as he shared about the wonder of this call to live as a missionary disciple, he became friends with Dr. John Love. The contagion of the Holy Spirit brought them together in the hope that this book would encourage many others to live as friends and companions of the risen Jesus. In writing this book, they have lived, and invite us to live, in the truth of what Pope Benedict taught us:

> Only where God is seen does life truly begin. Only when we meet the living God in Christ do we know what life is. We are not some casual and meaningless product of evolution. Each of us is the result of a thought of God. Each of us is willed, each of us is loved, and each of us is necessary. . . . There is nothing more beautiful than to know him and to speak to others of our friendship with him.[2]

This speaking to others about our friendship with Jesus is the foundation for our call to proclaim his love and mercy to the family of nations in the New Evangelization. Through the great gift of this book and by exercising a lively faith, you will be given new graces to live in the awesome beauty of friendship with the risen Jesus.

In his apostolic exhortation *Evangelii Gaudium* [The Joy of the Gospel], Pope Francis said that the Lord was able to attract people by the way in which he looked at them, "seeing beyond their weaknesses and failings" (141). "Jesus' gaze, burning with love, expands to embrace all his people," he wrote. "If he speaks to someone, he looks into their eyes with deep love and concern" (268, 269).

Indeed, we become what we behold! With what this helpful book teaches us about evangelization, we can heed the call of Pope Francis to "go forth to offer everyone the life of Jesus Christ" (*Evangelii Gaudium*, 49). As the people of God, we learn to embrace everyone because we are the disciples of the One who knelt before his own to wash their feet (24).

I want to pray a blessing for you now. As you read this wonderful story, may you see yourself anew through the eyes of Jesus in the light of the Holy Spirit. May you see yourself as a new creation in Christ (2 Corinthians 5:17), a creation who is the Father's delight (Isaiah 62:4). May the boundaries of love expand in your heart to receive more joy as a missionary disciple of Jesus.

Fr. John Horn, SJ, D.Min.
Faculty, St. Vincent DePaul Seminary, Florida
Cofounder, Institute for Priestly Formation

Blazing a Trail

There are plenty of clubs, activities, and meetings that crowd a seminarian's schedule, so when several seminarians decided to start the New Evangelization Club at Mount St. Mary in Emmitsburg, Maryland, several years ago, they spread the news about the new club by word of mouth. Their fledgling club had just gotten the go-ahead for a mission trip to a college campus—George Mason University in Fairfax, Virginia—and they knew they would need to prepare. They wanted to be intentional and personal about gathering the group that would take the first mission trip for the club. In their thirty-minute meetings, they would practice giving their personal testimonies and how to approach people in gentle and disarming ways that would open the doors to conversion. They also realized that they would need to know more about what the Church had to say about evangelization and how to do it. So they asked me to speak to them.

I was already teaching a required course to the deacons in the seminary that included a unit on evangelization, so I was familiar with the documents and some resources for evangelization in the Catholic tradition. I put my thoughts together and prepared to summarize what I had learned for the members of the budding New Evangelization Club. I was teaching a class called "Evangelization and Conversion" that same semester, and I had done different kinds of evangelizing work for a number of years. After a quick prayer, I knew just what to tell the missionaries-in-training, and I still have the half sheet of paper on which I jotted my notes.

I told the guys about a Vatican II document specifically on evangelization, in which the Council fathers instruct newly formed local Church communities to send out missionaries early in their development and growth. You might think that new groups of Christians should mature in their faith, develop support structures, and instruct new members for years before thinking of sending people out to share the faith. But the joy and exuberance of new converts is a priceless gift, and the bishops at Vatican II encouraged the newly formed Catholic communities to share this treasure (*Ad Gentes*, 20–21).

Next, I pointed the men to Paul VI's exhortation on evangelization, *Evangelii Nuntiandi* (which means, "Evangelization Today"). Blessed Pope Paul VI wrote in 1975 that the whole Christian community needs to evangelize, preaching Christ and trusting in the Holy Spirit, who gives life and drives conversion. Paul VI especially encouraged the laity and the clergy to work together in the essential mission and identity of the Church: to make Christ present in the world for the salvation of all people. Although St. John Paul II usually gets credit for announcing the "New Evangelization," Paul VI was focused on evangelization and already proclaiming it years before Pope John Paul entered the world stage. Of course, I did speak about John Paul's *Novo Millennio Ineunte* [At the

Beginning of the New Millennium], one of the many documents in which John Paul called for and explained the New Evangelization.

As Fr. Thomas explains later, St. John Paul spends the majority of that letter calling Christians to "contemplate the face of Christ" as the practical means of preparing for mission. I pointed out to the guys that he also offers a blueprint for evangelization according to the vision of the Church outlined at Vatican II. John Paul wrote that each parish should become a "school of prayer," where lay parishioners can develop a deep, transformative relationship with Christ. The pastor should be the "dean of the school," teaching and guiding his people. This means that the pastor must first delve into the deepest mysteries of Christian prayer himself so that he might be able to lead and teach his parishioners. John Paul mentioned St. Teresa of Avila and St. John of the Cross as good examples and resources for understanding just how deeply and fully God wants to engage each and every Christian. He wrote that each Christian receives this calling and the gifts to respond generously to it through their baptism. I think that struck an important note for the seminarians because, first, they themselves, as baptized persons, had a responsibility to pursue the Lord and respond to his call to holiness, even though they were not yet ordained. Second, realizing the high calling of the baptized gave them different expectations for the people they would meet on college campuses and in later parish missions.

After sharing these and other thoughts and some follow-up resources, I asked the guys if they would like to hear my three-minute testimony, and they immediately agreed. I told them about my Catholic upbringing, the challenge of my parents' messy divorce, and my journey to the point when, at a Steubenville Youth Conference during exposition of the Blessed Sacrament, I knelt and prayed, "I want to fall in love with you" over and over again. Jesus answered my prayer marvelously that night and began leading me ever deeper into his love.

My talk and testimony gave the men the material to work with and an awareness of the recent guidance of the Church on evangelization, and they took the initiative in putting this together with elements of their own training (some had been missionaries with FOCUS, the Fellowship of Catholic University Students) and their collected experiences of evangelization to get ready for the upcoming mission trip.

Training for Missionaries

For that first mission trip, we really felt like we were blazing a trail, so we tried as best we could to get ready for whatever was going to happen when we stepped on campus at George Mason. We ended up with four talks at the Mount: "Contemplating the Face of Christ," "Personal Testimony," "Kerygma" (about the fundamental gospel message that we wanted to share), and "How to Win Friends and Influence People for Christ." Chapters 3 through 6 of this book come out of those core training sessions in preparation for our first mission trip. The more times we went on the trips, however, the more seminarians got involved in planning and preparing the missionaries, which turned out to be a great blessing because different guys added great material or ways of presenting it that improved and polished up our pretrip formation.

We presented ideas from Sherry Weddell's book *Forming Intentional Disciples* about the "thresholds of conversion" to give the guys tools to recognize where someone is in their spiritual journey and tips about how to help people take the next step along that road. At the same time, I was teaching the evangelization class about St. Teresa of Avila's spiritual classic, *Interior Castle*. It was amazing to discover that many of the new tools in Sherry's book had roots going back to St. Teresa. The men asked me to return to our weekly meeting to share St. Teresa's insights about the stages of spiritual growth with all of the missionaries in training.

Both Fr. Thomas and I also instructed guys about how to approach people of different Christian denominations and other religious traditions. We told them not to bring up uncomfortable or contentious questions, such as talking about violence and religion with Muslims. Instead, we suggested that guys draw attention to the riches in the Catholic tradition that such people do not have in their own faith. This would give us the chance to talk about the great things we have as Catholics, like the sacraments for example, with the hope that others would at least be curious about them and find them attractive and life-giving.

In the days just before our work on campus, we took the time to train the guys in very practical methods for the evangelizing conversations that we wanted to have on the mission trips. Given our plan to go out two by two, the way Jesus sent out his disciples in the Gospels, we worked on how to coordinate with one's partner.

This book, then, is a summary of what we have learned together. (Fr. Thomas will tell the story in his voice, although we have collaborated on the entire book. Both the introduction and the conclusion are in my voice.) The book outlines the talks and training we used in the New Evangelization Club for how to evangelize. First, we can't make disciples unless we are disciples ourselves. We realized that our initial step to becoming effective missionaries was to prayerfully contemplate Christ and his love. Then we learned how to proclaim the kerygma— the essential gospel message. We also practiced how to share our personal testimonies, how to initiate evangelizing conversations, and how to bring people to the place where they ask Jesus to come into their lives. We learned about the advantage of going out on campuses in teams, two by two, just like the apostles. Finally, we learned to spend time on-site, once we arrived, in prayer, beseeching the Holy Spirit to fill us so that we could proclaim Christ's love. We want to share all that we have learned with you so that you might be empowered to do what we have done—to share Christ with those who so desperately need to hear the Good News.

Dr. John D. Love, STD
Fr. Thomas Cavanaugh

CHAPTER 1

The Founding of the New Evangelization Club

I had sent my application to the seminary, and I was feeling overjoyed—but also anxious. So when the phone call from the vocations director came, my heart was pounding. He said, "The bishop has just officially accepted you as a seminarian for our diocese, and you will begin seminary this August." I calmly responded, "Oh, great! Thanks be to God." "Yes, thanks be to God," replied my vocations director. "You will be sent where I went, Mount St. Mary's Seminary in Emmitsburg, Maryland."

Although excited and relieved when I finally knew that I was entering the seminary, I still found it difficult to embrace the idea of six more years of school. I wanted to be a priest and start preaching and teaching right away! That's true of many of the seminarians, but by the time we get our things unpacked in our new room in the seminary, we settle down a little bit. A happy thought comes to us that Jesus and the Church have been doing this for two thousand years, and they know a lot better than we do about what they are doing and how to form men for the priesthood. So we are given a formation adviser, and we choose a spiritual director from the priests in the house. We go with the program, try to be as generous as possible, and hope to be "ready enough" for the sacramental and pastoral work that God is calling us to do. As it's often said, God doesn't call the equipped; he equips the called.

I was born and raised in the Arlington Diocese just outside of Washington, DC, and was ordained in 2013, the Year of Faith, for the priesthood in my diocese. The formation I received in those six years, and surely what I have learned from family, friends, parishioners, and teachers throughout my life, also prepared me to be a priest of the New Evangelization. The New Evangelization, in fact, colors every aspect of formation in seminary and now stands as the billboard of the Church and its backdrop. Every diocese across the nation and the world is discovering this deepest identity of the Church. We who were ordained in the Year of Faith will not have been ordained for the continuation of the maintenance of a Church already established. Rather, we have been awakened to the reality that the Church exists to evangelize. I cannot, I must not, live as a mere sacramental custodian in a parish of northern Virginia. You and I, priest and lay, exist to evangelize, to be Christ's witnesses and to proclaim the gospel in and to the world.

The story of this book and the practical tools and examples of what we have done during our time as seminarians begins about two and a half years into my formation. In what is called "First Theology," we took a course on Christian spirituality, and I felt a desire emerge within me to go on a thirty-day Ignatian silent retreat. My diocese sent me to Omaha, Nebraska, where the Institute for Priestly Formation holds a summer program of spiritual formation and offers thirty-day silent retreats using the traditional Ignatian Spiritual Exercises. There were many graces from the retreat, but I was especially convicted that I had not been evangelizing and sensed that both God and the Church were calling me and everyone else to be more deliberate in our efforts to do so. How or what, I did not know. Nevertheless, something had to be done, something had to get started to fulfill this call of the New Evangelization.

Upon returning to the seminary the following August, now in Second Theology, I went to my first formation-advising meeting with Fr. Brett Brannen of the Savannah, Georgia, diocese, who was then vice-rector of the Mount. He is also well known for his truly spectacular work in vocations and wrote probably one of the most effective guides for discernment to the priesthood, *To Save a Thousand Souls*.[3] Those who have heard him speak or who have lived with him know that he has a fantastic Southern accent, which makes his already loving and gentle personality that much kinder. Nevertheless, even when it was absolutely clear what he had said in spite of his accent, the rector would joke, "Can we get a translator in here?" Anyway, as we got to the end of our meeting, he stopped me and said with his Georgian priestly smile, "Now, Thomas, you've been here for three years now, and I want you to know that you're doing very well. Son, you're going to be a fine priest indeed; you know what I mean?" He often ends sentences with a question. "I've got a different kind of question than you're probably used to here, but I want you to be honest, and don't have any worries—just tell me what you feel is the right thing in your heart to say. You get what I'm asking you? In your prayerful, humble opinion, what, if anything, do you think needs to be changed, improved, or added to formation here at this wonderful institution of Mount St. Mary's? Anything at all?"

If any other priest in formation had asked that, I would have been a little nervous, but Fr. Brannen's soothing Southern drawl and kindly Christlike personality gave me the peace and confidence to respond quite openly. However, though unafraid, I did feel a bit like a deer in the headlights. It wasn't clear to me if this was a standard question that was asked that year or if it was just a humble priest that desired to know my opinion. It is certainly not on the radar for us in formation to be giving suggestions or corrections of how better to form us. I'm sure I dumbly blinked my eyes for about a minute or so. Yet even with my brain not firing on all cylinders, words began to come out of my mouth and I said, "Well, I felt on my thirty-day silent retreat this summer that I should make a more serious effort to evangelize. And it always inspired me to think of Jesus' formation of the twelve apostles and the seventy-two disciples as the very thing we are getting here at the Mount. Jesus sent his seminarians out two by two to get some experience in evangelization before he ascended to the Father."

"What are you saying then, Thomas? Do we need to do something like that here at the Mount?" Realizing what I had said, I autocorrected. "Well, uh, I don't know if we necessarily need to do that, but what if I and some other seminarians did something like that some time? Would that be okay?"

"Oh sure, Thomas, I'd be more than happy to see you guys going out and talking to people about Jesus our Savior. Just as long as you clear it with me and the seminary before you do it, that sounds just fine to me!"

Lightning Strikes

Leaving the meeting a bit confused about what had just happened, I went to the chapel to pray about what this might mean. Over the next few days and weeks, I began to talk to my brother seminarians, and we all started to daydream together about what to do. Though we were still unclear, we decided to start meeting each week for an hour to pray together and talk about evangelization. At the same time, I was taking a course on evangelization with Dr. John Love, and he suggested that we read and discuss the documents from the course in these meetings. Seminarians are usually fairly overwhelmed with academics, so we decided to spread out the work. Each of us would read a document and then give an overview in the meetings as a prompt for discussion. The two documents that stood out the most were *Evangelii Nuntiandi* by Blessed Pope Paul VI and *Novo Millennio Ineunte* by Pope St. John Paul II.

The phrase "the gospel must be preached" seemed to be repeated again and again in these documents. We realized that we could not just rely on the popular adage attributed to St. Francis of Assisi: "Preach always, and if necessary, use words." The documents were clear that words needed to be used, and they quoted St. Paul, who said that the gospel "is the power of God for the salvation of everyone who believes" (Romans

1:16), as well as "Woe to me if I do not preach [the gospel]" (1 Corinthians 9:16) and "How can they believe in him of whom they have not heard? And how can they hear without someone to preach?" (Romans 10:14). These are very convicting words because so few of us have ever "preached the gospel" to nonbelievers. In fact, simply to talk about faith in public seems like it would be most unwelcome in our society today.

Well, we got to the end of the semester, and though very inspired and convicted that we needed to do something, we still did not know what to do. Then one day I was talking with my good buddy Thomas Gallagher (also from the Arlington Diocese) about how much we had enjoyed mixing vacations with mission trips. We had gone on a mission trip with a group of college students to the Dominican Republic during the prior spring break, and rather than being more exhausted for the rest of our semester, we were more invigorated to study and pray harder. That was due not primarily to the adventure of overseas travel but to the conversations we had and the conversions we saw in the students. Plus, our failures to give satisfying answers to their questions motivated us to seek to know God and our faith better. "What if this coming spring break, we did just what Jesus did with the seventy-two disciples?" Thomas suggested. "YES!" I responded. "Let's go to a local college for a week and just start up conversations with people about Jesus and Catholicism." Lightning had struck! "We can go to George Mason University," Thomas said. He had graduated from there just a few years back and knew the campus minister well, and the main campus is in Fairfax, Virginia—our own diocese.

In our next gathering of what had come to be called the "New Evangelization Club," Thomas and I pitched the idea. We would go down to the college the first Saturday of our break, get the lay of the land, talk to the students involved in campus ministry, and have the other seminarians join us on campus for three days of conversations with their peers about Jesus and the faith. "It's a simple plan," said Thomas. "We'll go two by two, in the same way that Jesus sent out his seventy-two disciples." It really was simple, but that made it really practical and easy to sell. The other guys in the group all agreed that it was a good idea.

We told Fr. Brannen and got the go-ahead from the seminary. Then we started to spread the word, and in a few days we had twenty-five guys signed up to go. We called the campus ministry, and they were interested but wanted assurance that the guys had been well formed for doing such a thing before they would give an approval. We assured them that the seminarians would be trained to be gentle, loving, and nonconfrontational. This was enough for them, and we got the thumbs up.

Having read the doctrine, we were ready for the practical tools and guidelines so that we could start training up the seminarians. So we asked around among the professors and discovered that there really wasn't any kind of manual, guide, or program to do such a thing. FOCUS, the Fellowship of Catholic University Students (which Thomas, I, and several other seminarians in the New Evangelization Club had belonged to before seminary) had good tools—but the materials were mostly for long-term discipleship relationships. Evangelicals seemed to have guidance on how to convert people in a five-minute conversation. We were looking for something in the middle.

What we ended up doing was compiling a plethora of models of discipleship and evangelization to produce the program that this book presents in the following chapters. Though interiorly fearful, we knew that the Spirit was with us. I think that everyone else thought that we had some "official manual" and were professional, fearless evangelists.

Honestly, we expected to be chewed up and spit out like the first martyrs sent to the lions. We were told before going out that many GMU students were quite pagan and fairly hostile to religious people. Many seminarians who did not join us on that trip were skeptical about any success, and I had my doubts about it as well. The result was quite the opposite. During those three and a half days on campus, we spoke with well over seven hundred students, and there was only one person who picked a fight with one of us—who happened to be me. There was some apathy, but by and large, the seminarians had long, pleasant, and productive conversations.

We had planned a larger event on the concluding night—something we could invite people to when we talked with them. It was well attended, but 90 percent of the people were probably campus ministry students who had been around awhile. However, we know for sure that there were at least ten new students that night, two of whom were not Catholic and one who came into the Church and still e-mails me. There were a few fallen-away Catholics who returned to the faith, and the FOCUS missionaries who work with the

Catholic campus ministry there reported that the Catholic students were talking about the seminarians for months after our mission. Since then, the seminarians have gone back to do more missions at GMU.

The Lost Sheep

Perhaps one convert is not very impressive for conversations with more than seven hundred students. I was happy with it. Jesus is the Good Shepherd who leaves the ninety-nine to go after the one lost sheep. But what was objectively impressive was the change that came about in us, the evangelizing seminarians. We discovered something new about ourselves from this three-day trip. While evangelizing, we were happier than we perhaps had ever been in our lives. We were completely exhausted but didn't want to leave. We came back to the Mount after the trip and gathered in fellowship to share all the stories from our conversations with students and to read together from Luke's Gospel how Jesus responded to the return of the disciples from their missionary journey: "He rejoiced in the holy Spirit" (10:21). This evangelization experience left us with an indescribable joy, as if we were experiencing the delight of our Lord for us.

This is not the end of the story! With this same enthusiasm, we went back to GMU the following semester, and a good number of those conversations and conversions that were started in our first trip were brought further along, and there were several more conversions. This led to a third trip, this time to

Georgia Southern University in Statesboro. It took quite a bit more driving to get to this school, but it was well worth it. Fr. Brannen, who had transferred there as chaplain for a time, gave us a very warm welcome with true Southern hospitality, literally inviting us into his own home. We have experienced such great generosity from the Church everywhere we've gone; people feel the joy and enthusiasm at work in the evangelist. In Georgia we added two things that made a big difference: we had a tent set up on the middle of campus with Eucharistic Adoration going on throughout the day, and we had the closing event in one of the main auditoriums on campus. Almost one hundred students who were not part of campus ministry or FOCUS came to this event, and the FOCUS missionaries planned to start ten new Bible study groups as a result. One of those Bible studies was with a group of students from the LBGT alliance, several of whom had conversions to Catholicism as a result.

The next trip was to Ball State in Indiana, during which we added another event, a Eucharistic procession through the campus. There seemed to be a sense of darkness on that campus, and the apathy was staunch. Nevertheless, there were some amazing conversions there as well, and I believe four Bible study groups were started. We also visited James Madison University in Harrisonburg, Virginia, and the stories that the seminarians told upon returning from there were absolutely amazing!

By the time I was ordained, we had spoken to somewhere between 3,000 to 6,000 college students. About 500 or less of those conversations included conflict, argument, or a complete lack of interest. About one in one hundred of those we have spoken to come to the big events, and one in five of those who come stick around to join Bible studies and to learn more about the faith. Many return to or convert to Catholicism. To be sure, we did not keep a strict count on the numbers; we kept track by counting e-mails and fliers and Bibles left over, along with the numbers that seminarians gave to us at the end of each trip. However, even if we are off by a few hundred here or there, we have not learned any less. It's not only about the numbers; it's about the living encounter with Jesus Christ!

One thing we have learned again and again: it is a complete fallacy that people find it impolite to talk about religion. They *love* to talk about religion. They will talk for hours about religion. They love hearing and talking to people who are excited about their faith! They love to talk about Jesus; the reason that no one usually talks about him is because no one knows him. They have so many questions and opinions that they want clarified or confirmed from people that do know him and are living their Catholic faith. People love being loved the way only disciples of Jesus can love. They are totally shocked and impressed that we who have the most controversial opinions in our nation have the courage and desire to come out into the world to put ourselves on the line in hopes that Jesus would be known.

And so, what follows is what we have learned about going out to proclaim the gospel.

CHAPTER 2

What Does It Mean to Be a Disciple of Christ?

For to me life is Christ, and death is gain.
(Philippians 1:21)

When I first started to follow Christ, I had been a baptized Catholic for almost nineteen years. To be more specific, I had been alive for eighteen years, ten months, and two days, and yet spiritually, I had not yet begun to be alive—because I had not yet made a conscious choice to follow Christ. When I began to believe that Jesus truly is who he claims to be in the Gospels, the grace I had received at baptism was activated in my soul through faith, and I began to thrive spiritually. I had no one around me to explain to me what had happened. All I knew was that something was drastically different. Everything had become more beautiful somehow; people were far more interesting, and when I looked into myself, I saw deep within me another Person—Jesus Christ.

The experience of being alive in Christ was new and wonderful, and I could see right away that I was being formed into a much more loving, generous person. Jesus was revealing to me the Father and, at the same time, myself. What I realized was that at the core of my being was the Triune God; the source of life was now my life.

The experience of coming alive in Christ immediately compelled me to share that love in community and with those who had not yet been awakened to the peace, love, and joy that can be born in us through cooperation with the grace of the Holy Spirit. I felt as if I were the student of Jesus, and he was teaching me mysteriously from within my own heart. Fairly quickly, I realized this was normal for someone who has been awakened to Christ through faith; it was normal to experience these two movements of the Holy Spirit. The first movement is to turn inward to find Christ. The second is to turn outward, to see the world and people differently and to share and to give to others that experience of the living God. The way of discipleship is at once an encounter with the divinity and the humanity of Jesus Christ and a spiritual compulsion to *become* the encounter of Jesus Christ for others.

Unfortunately, my past behavior, habits, and attitudes began to reemerge as the powerful sense of God's presence became normal and even more as that feeling of spiritual vigor became dimmed. Spiritual life was also a battle, and it has proven to be a continual dying and rising with Christ. Failure, repentance, and resurrection are a daily, weekly, and yearly experience.

Nevertheless, I wondered if it was possible to reawaken that transcendent sensation of the supernatural in such a way as to not only be alive in Christ but also to thrive in him. What I initially experienced was like putting the right sort of gasoline in the tank. What would it be like, I wondered, to run at all times on all cylinders? To be free and fully alive?

The School of Discipleship

Early on in my conversion, my Protestant friends invited me to join them as a missionary in Ethiopia and, while there, to learn the discipleship model of Young Life in the leadership program for evangelization designed and led by Chuck Reinhold. Chuck is not a Catholic, but everything I learned from Chuck is also why I am still a Catholic, and it was really with him that I began to seriously consider the call to the priesthood. Before I explain all that he taught me about Catholicism, I will share with you the basic program that Chuck used to help those he was forming as disciples, disciple makers, and evangelists.

What you see is a version of what is called the "Wheel of Discipleship." It has been used by so many different Protestant groups that it is hard to say which one can really take credit for it. It is often attributed to The Navigators, an international organization established in 1933 that provides a good number of tools for catechizing disciples to make it easy and clear as to what is expected and what is necessary for a follower of Christ. The idea is that in order to keep Christ as the center of your life, you must spend time every day praying, reading the word of God, gathering in fellowship with other believers, and living as a witness of Christ in your day-to-day life.

We learned about the Wheel of Discipleship by doing it. Chuck required that we all wake up every day at 5 a.m. and spend the morning praying and reading the Scriptures until about 8 a.m. Then twice each week all of the disciples (about fifteen of us) would gather together to pray and reflect on the word of God together. Chuck would always point out to us how much joy we had in these times of fellowship, and after a month or so, he told us his secret: "God made us to love him and to love each other. My goal for every Tuesday and Thursday gathering, no matter what materials we are going over, is to help you all to love God and love each other. That's what fills you up to go out to evangelize—your growing friendship with Christ and with each other in Christ!" After these meetings, we, ecstatic with joy, would go out to our assignments to start up friendships for Christ.

The other disciples in this group seemed to have had an encounter with Christ that was similar to mine. What I learned from this twice-a-week fellowship was that the spiritual compulsion I had experienced from day one is actually Jesus' response to anyone who asks about how one attains eternal life. Jesus always responds that the greatest commandment is this: "You shall love the Lord, your God, with all your heart, with all your soul, and with all your mind. This is the greatest and the first commandment. The second is like it: You shall love your neighbor as yourself" (Matthew 22:37-39). What I learned from Chuck was how specifically to love God and others. It is this that I call the "school of discipleship."

Discipleship: The Catholic Understanding

Now, what is the Catholic way of discipleship? You may have noticed there are some things missing from the wheel above. The moral life, for one thing, is missing. Sacred Tradition and the interpretive guidance of the Magisterium and, most obvious of all, the sacraments are also missing. Besides Jesus himself, Chuck used St. Francis of Assisi as his example for teaching us how to live in the school of discipleship. He loved the symbolism of St. Francis stripping off his clothing and being embraced by the bishop's garment. We encounter Christ in the incarnational ministry of his body, the Church, wherein we grow in the life of charity; we learn how to interpret the word of God, and like St. Francis, we learn to be completely satisfied by the nourishment of the Eucharist.

Chuck would say, "Here was a man who could really say, 'I have been crucified with Christ, and it is no longer I who live but Christ lives in me. The life which I *now* live in Christ I live by faith in the Son of God who loves me and gave *everything* for me!'" (cf. Galatians 2:19-20). His point was that St. Francis was a real disciple. He had encountered the living Christ through the Church, had come to know him in prayer and the Scriptures, and had become utterly docile to his teachings.

I remember one time talking to Chuck at the lunch table, and one of my brother disciples was complaining about how so many Christians had become so worldly and how many pastors and ministers were to blame. (It may have been around the time that the Episcopalian Church was allowing for active homosexuals to be ordained.) "Well, there is one denomination that has always stood its ground. Which one might that be, Tommy-boy?" He glanced at me with a twinkle in his eye. "The Catholic Church is the only one that holds to the Gospel on the moral teaching of Christ."

Not long after that, in a private meeting with Chuck, I was telling him about my growing desire to become a Catholic priest. "There are a lot of things that I love about the Catholic Church. God knows I've learned so much about discipleship from St. Francis and those Jesuit guys. You're going to be the best priest I know," he said, pausing, and then he looked at me and added, "if you teach those Catholics discipleship."

Chuck is a simple man and one of the most amazing disciples I have ever met. I'm not sure, however, if he realized how very prophetic his words were. We as Catholics have all the elements of discipleship, and we faithfully "do" discipleship every day. But if you asked one hundred Catholics after Mass on any given Sunday, "Are you a disciple of Jesus Christ?" it is likely that less than 3 percent of them would answer in the affirmative. The very unfortunate reality is that the vast majority of Christians of any flavor in America would not honestly be able to answer yes to that question. Most of them could not even tell you what it means to be in a relationship with Jesus Christ. I personally have asked more than one thousand Catholics and Christians after Mass or in various settings, especially on mission trips to college campuses, "Has anyone ever shown you how to have a relationship with Jesus Christ?" or "Have you ever read for yourself what Jesus himself says about how to have a relationship with God?" So far, less than twenty people have answered yes, and even those who did say yes, when prodded further, really didn't know what they had just said yes to.

Reality Check and Positive Discipleship

Almost Christian: What The Faith of Our Teenagers Is Telling the American Church is the title of a recent book that interprets the findings of several years of research on the religious faith of the youth in America.[4] Based on a survey of several thousand high school and college students as well as face-to-face interviews, the author, Princeton Theological Seminary professor Kendra Creasy Dean, discovered was that the vast majority of self-described Christians (this includes Catholics) were in fact not quite what they thought they were. Their understanding of Christianity could be described more accurately as a *moralistic, therapeutic deism*. Why did they believe this? Because that is what their parents believe and taught them. Why do their parents believe this? Because that is what they understand their pastors, priests, and ministers to be teaching and living. It is a statistical fact that Catholics are not only missing it; what they are getting is a very complex and insidious heresy.

Sherry Weddell, the author of *Forming Intentional Disciples*, offers a swath of statistics that lead her to a similar conclusion. There is a disconnect between the current norm in Catholic parishes and what the Church says is normal about the Christian life. Weddell found many people who serve in their parishes but who have had no conscious relationship with God; they are not "intentional disciples."[5] She describes the traits and activities of "intentional disciples," but she does not systematically present an outline of the necessary elements of Christian discipleship. Her aim is to help parishes inspire parishioners to consciously choose Christian discipleship as a way of revitalizing the Church.

Weddell offers helpful direction about how to help people make the choice to be a disciple, especially in her explanation of the "thresholds of conversion." She presents five thresholds in the process of moving from a curious inquirer to an intentional disciple who seeks the Lord. Based on her vast experience at thousands of parishes across the US, she helps the reader identify where people are in this process (which threshold are they at or approaching?) and how to help them continue in the path of conversion. Generally speaking, people simply do not become "intentional disciples" without some help and direction. They need to be led into it.[6]

The most exhaustive data on the state of the Catholic parish was done by the Dynamic Catholic Institute under the leadership of Matthew Kelly.[7] What he discovered about the disciples of our parishes, which he calls "dynamic Catholics," is that they compose just fewer than 7 percent of the average congregation. These Catholics are the ones who show signs of being authentic followers of Christ; according to Kelly, they exhibit four signs: prayer, study, generosity, and evangelization. While small in number, he found that this little flock was amazingly productive, accomplishing roughly 85 percent of all the ministry in the Church community and any outreach of the parish. It is important to note that the priests of these parishes seemed to know about these people—"the same fifty people" in every parish who do everything—but do not know why they are so engaged.

These are the disciples already made, but what about the disciple makers? Msgr. Stephen Rossetti also did one of the most extensive studies on the Church, but he was most interested in the priests: the disciple makers. He discovered that the majority of priests are happier than the average American. The title of the book reveals what he also discovered: *Why Priests Are Happy.*[8] As in any study, there is a spectrum, even in the cream of the crop. I reduced his findings on the spiritual dimension of priesthood to basically five factors that account for why happy priests are happy: (1) their relationship with Jesus Christ is the center of their life; (2) they have brother priest and perhaps also lay friends who also place their relationship with Christ at the center; (3) the aim of all their ministry is to help people develop a relationship with Christ and to gather them together even as they (the priests) do with their brother priests; (4) they feel compelled by God through their superiors, their bishop, to do the above three things; (5) they triage by making the first three factors the priority and goal of every task or ministry in the parish, and they are willing to delegate or to cut programs that are not for this purpose.

If the priests do all five of the above, they are outliers even among the priests who are in a technical sense the happiest. Every priest who is happy has each of these factors to some degree at play in their lives, but the happiest—those who are fully and faithfully doing all five—are the most effective. I look at a priest like Fr. Bret Brannen as a prime example of this happy and effective priest disciple. Why are they happy and why are they effective? It is because they are living the life of discipleship—whether they call it that or not.

These elements seem to be repeating themselves in the research, but how do they square with Scripture and Tradition? Erasmo Leiva-Merikakis, one of the most eloquent of Catholic Scripture scholars, wrote an excellent book called *The Way of the Disciple*. (Since then he has joined the Cistercians and is known as Fr. Simeon.) Leiva-Merikakis identifies five elements that he draws from this single passage: "He went up the mountain and summoned those whom he wanted and they came to him. He appointed twelve [whom he also named apostles] that they might be with him and he might send them forth to preach and to have authority to drive out demons"

(Mark 3:13-15). In this passage, Jesus "gives us the whole structure of authentic discipleship in a nutshell." Leiva-Merikakis sees there five elements: "(1) our solitude with Jesus; (2) his freedom in choosing and calling; (3) our response to the call; (4) the shared life of companionship with Jesus and the other disciples; and (5) the mission to teach and heal." It is not just because he was discerning monastic life that he adds this: "Of these five elements, only the fifth involves any visible activity in the world; the other four are interior work and represent the substantial center of the disciple's experience, with the visible apostolate as fruit."[9] Notice also that Leiva-Merikakis' biblically conceived way of discipleship is almost identical to what Rossetti has discovered that makes a priest so happy.

It is interesting to note the similarities and the differences of these books, which have been some of the most popular and/or most profound on the subject of Catholic discipleship in the last ten years. They all mention prayer or a relationship with Christ, and they all mention evangelization. There is interestingly very little mention by way of the importance of the sacraments, the life of obedience and virtue, and the *communio* of the gatherings with the body of Christ. The only one that mentions all three of these things also discovered that these three, along with prayer, study, and evangelization, are essential for the happiness of the priests as disciples. However, the things that account for the happiness of the priest are necessary for the happiness of every human person. Vatican II's *Lumen Gentium* makes this very clear in the pronouncement of the "universal call to holiness" (5). All the baptized are called to this happiness, and that is why the Council fathers used interchangeably the designations "the baptized" and "the disciples of Jesus Christ." All the baptized need to understand themselves as disciples of Jesus Christ and learn that for the disciple to be truly happy in this life, seven elements are necessary. What are these elements?

The Seven Pillars of Catholic Discipleship

Living and thriving disciples must be (1) intentionally *Christocentric*, which means they (2) have daily *prayer*; (3) live in *obedience* to Christ and the Church; (4) have a plan for the *study* and contemplation of the deposit of faith, his *word*; (5) live in the *sacramental mystery*; (6) experience *communion*, which is lived out in a tight-knit community; and (7) walk with Jesus in the world as his witness through *evangelization*.

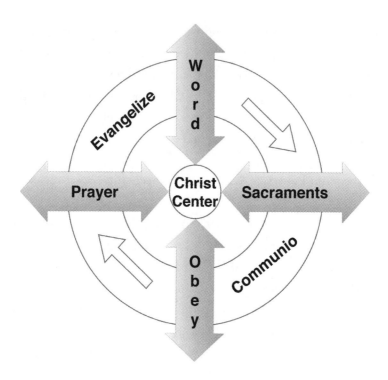

The model above is the image I first proposed to the New Evangelization Club for an initial understanding of the theology of discipleship. Since then, I have developed it quite a bit, but for the purposes of this book, this is quite sufficient. All the seven pillars of discipleship are essential to the nature of being a baptized follower of Jesus Christ. If one element is not active or not growing, then the disciple is not going to be thriving, plain and simple. Evangelization is as important as prayer to the spiritual and human health of the disciple, because each pillar is integral to the integrity of the structure of intimacy with the Person of Jesus Christ.

What Does This Mean for Evangelization?

Putting all of this together, we can understand what Pope Benedict XVI said in 2002 when he was still Cardinal Ratzinger: that evangelization is simply teaching others the "art of living," and discipleship is the human relationship by which we gradually make ourselves open to the man "who is Life."[10] Only inasmuch as we live the life of discipleship will we be effective and able to evangelize. Yet the opposite is equally true: even if we have only just begun to live the happy life of discipleship, we are already able to evangelize. Furthermore, we will only really be living the joy of discipleship if we evangelize. And the implication of Ratzinger's definition of evangelization is that we are only really living if we are teaching others how to live.

Discipleship is a particular kind of relationship with Jesus by which we experience the humanity of Christ as his first followers did. It is how we as individual followers come to know him: by walking with him in our lives and in the Church as we move toward eternal happiness, where we will see God face-to-face and know him "as [we are] fully known" (1 Corinthians 13:12). From the moment of his ascension until now, the human communication and intimacy that the apostles experienced has not diminished, though it did change—it was perfected. The first disciples were blinded by their senses to varying degrees, which put a barrier between their deepest core and the second divine Person, the incarnate Word. When Jesus ascended into heaven, he then sent the Holy Spirit to dwell "with" them and also "in" them (John 14:17). They discovered that he was present with them in a new way, an interior way, and yet the human aspects of their relationship also deepened. Now when they spoke to him, they were filled with the power of Jesus' presence in the deepest core of their being—in their intellects and wills, in their appetites, and even in their bodies and their fellowship. When they went out to proclaim him, they went with him because he was in them, and they really *were* him to others. So also with you and me.

While my initial experience of becoming alive in Christ was a crucial beginning, I now see how also to thrive in Christ: discipleship. I see so many Catholics who do not know what they have received from the sacraments. As I noted above, to be baptized and to be a disciple of Christ are synonyms in the language of the Vatican II Council fathers. If you are a baptized Catholic, you have a tremendous treasure within you. You are a great danger to the armies of darkness and the lies of the world. You also are in great danger yourself if you do not have all of these pillars of discipleship activated in a living relationship with Jesus. So now, let me show you, step-by-step, how we at Mount St. Mary's Seminary accomplished this.

CHAPTER 3

Contemplating the Face of Christ: The Key to Discipleship and Evangelization

A fter we decided that we were actually going to go out and boldly fulfill this calling in our hearts to proclaim the gospel, we realized that we didn't really know where to start. We had been inspired by reading most of the documents on evangelization from the twentieth century. Blessed Pope Paul VI's *Evangelii Nuntiandi* moved us most of all when it said that the Church "exists in order to evangelize" (14). But what does the Church say about how to prepare oneself and how to train and prepare others for evangelization? Sure, I could just teach from my prior experience, but that was not a satisfying option. At the time, I was taking a class with Dr. Love on evangelization, and he pointed me to Pope St. John Paul II's document *Novo Millennio Ineunte*, which he described as the pope's practical document on evangelization.

So I began to read it—very excitedly, I might add—because I was finally reading the "how-to" manual of the Church on evangelization. I got a few pages into the document. "*Duc in altum*," "Cast into the deep," the Holy Father kept saying. Yet I then became concerned when he went on for most of the document about "contemplating the face of Christ" without getting to the practical. In fact, it's not until the last few pages that he finally explains a few practical things that we could do if we are going to evangelize. To say the least, I was very disappointed and, quite honestly, irritated. Is there really no document of the Church, no manual, no practical guide for how to fulfill what *Evangelii Nuntiandi* says is the Church's deepest identity? I complained to Dr. Love, and again he said that *Novo Millennio Ineunte* was what I was looking for.

I decided to read it again. This time, however, I was going to read it on my knees before the tabernacle. The Lord knew my frustration, and I think my frustration is the frustration of many Catholics, both priest and lay, who wonder, *"Why does the Church keeps telling us to do this? And how do we do evangelization?"*

An Epiphany

So I prayed through this rather short document by John Paul II, which he wrote in the spring of the Jubilee Year 2000—promulgated at the very same time as my conversion, almost to the day. That was powerful enough to get my attention. The words were obviously exactly the same this second time around, only now I was praying through it. The Spirit was leading me, so it was hitting me on a different level. I had no expectations; I was ready to receive the word revealed in the Holy Spirit spoken through the Church.

"Duc in altum," "cast into the deep," "cast into the deep," "cast into the deep"! How do you cast into the deep? And what was St. John Paul really trying to get at? Did he mean to just

go for it, just go out and start shouting out the gospel on the highways and byways? Or was he saying something different? What waters was he suggesting we cast into?

Reading on, it began to talk about contemplating the face of Christ. Paragraph after paragraph on this subject, and for the life of me, I couldn't get it. "When will this become practical?" I asked myself.

Suddenly the lights turned on. The Holy Spirit has a way of doing that with me—I'm not the sharpest spoon in the drawer, and so he has to put the pieces together for me from time to time. *Contemplating the face of Christ is the most practical and the most necessary foundation for all the work of evangelization!* By contemplating the face of Christ, we cast ourselves more deeply into the waters of our own baptism. We can go more and more deeply into the grace we receive there and allow ourselves to be transformed by him in ways that we could never do ourselves. St. Paul speaks of these baptismal depths: "I have been crucified with Christ; yet I live, no longer I, but Christ lives in me; insofar as I now live in the flesh, I live by faith in the Son of God who has loved me and given himself up for me" (Galatians 2:19-20).

In other words, the nature of the Church to evangelize is not expressed in an activity, or at least not in some sort of "new program" (*Novo Millennio Ineunte*, 29). It is because we are transformed by Christ and incorporated into his life that we can share in his work of proclaiming the good news. Salvation history didn't end with Jesus' death or resurrection. The gift of the Holy Spirit at Pentecost made it possible for Christ to continue *his work of evangelization* in us as members of his own body. Therefore, it is imminently practical to contemplate the face of Christ as the first, last, and constant step in evangelization. Evangelization is nothing if not making Christ present to the world.

How Practical Is This, Really?

There are certain people who really have the gift of making a sale. My good friend Rami Baalbaki (now Br. Seraphim Pio with the Franciscan Friars of the Renewal) is one of those people. Though he never lived there, his family is from the Middle East, where they say that certain merchants can "sell you sand in the desert." His own mother jokingly says this about him, and it's true! For example, I don't like fruits or vegetables; in particular, I do not like coconut or pineapple. When I was a kid, it drove my parents crazy, and even today my friends make fun of me for it. I will not eat pineapple, ever, under any circumstances—that is, unless I am with Rami.

One time I was at his house, and he was talking to me about these healthy shakes that he makes. He was licking his lips the whole time as he spoke about them and spontaneously started to pull out a blender and a bunch of vegetables and fruits and indiscriminately place them in the blender, laughing and smiling like he was about to eat chocolate cake. I had seen all that he put in the blender, and I knew that I did not have the taste buds for it, even if it was extremely healthy. Nevertheless, he finished blending, took a sip, and let out a yelp of sheer pleasure. Then he poured me a glass and said, "You've got to try this, bro! I'm not even kidding, you just—just drink, dude." I did not and do not like anything he put in the blender, and if anyone else had made it, I would have refused. I'm not sure why he is so convincing, but I took a sip and—I liked it! Well, maybe just a little. I don't even know why, but I drank the whole thing.

Most of the time when we think about evangelization, we think that we need to develop the perfect arguments, the perfect sales pitch, have the perfect circumstances, and perhaps a little bit of magic as the cherry on top—or at least a miraculous grace to help make us genius saints with the power to convert souls. Lord, is that too much to ask? What we have discovered after speaking to thousands of college students on college mission trips is that these gifts mean very little, and the more you try to "convert people" rather than trust in God, the less success you will have. Alternatively, if you contemplate the face of Christ and let yourself be more and more transformed by him, people will be drawn to you as inexplicably as I was to the vegetable smoothie. Rami uses his gift of convincing people on himself and others to do things that are good for them. Over the years he has certainly used this gift to convince me to pray much more than to eat in a healthy way. It is his opinion that there is nothing more important and spiritually healthy than to spend time in Eucharistic Adoration. It is said that St. Francis of Assisi would lick his lips for days after receiving the Eucharist. Rami has found this same experience in the Eucharist and, like the veggie drink, now uses his gift to convince himself to spend at least one hour in Adoration and to persuade others to do the same. The point here is that through contemplating the face of Christ, God baptized Rami's gift. But what about the majority of us who do not have the gift?

Another friend of mine you should know about is my good buddy Randy (not his real name). Randy, like most of us, does not have the unique gift of Rami. To be honest, Randy does not give one the sense that he's selling anything; even if he were selling water in the desert and you paid for it, you'd feel like he was giving it to you. Though his personality type and style are completely different from Rami, he is extremely compelling. He often appears to be focused elsewhere. Not just lacking guile, he is completely unconcerned about salesmanship. Why? Because, like Rami, he is focused on the most important thing: the face of Jesus.

On our second mission trip, Randy was standing by the entrance to the Johnson Center, the center of the GMU campus where students can buy food from different vendors. Most of the students go through that door in the course of their day. There were about thirty seminarians on campus, all wearing clerics and walking around, especially in that area, starting up conversations with students. Randy's teammate was in a conversation with a group of Muslims, and I was there as an observer to help give tips if I could. I watched sadly as Randy let himself be pushed out of the conversation by the strong personalities of his teammate and this Muslim student. He was just standing there, smiling, and I was standing in the path of the door, gearing up to talk to Randy to encourage him to stay in the conversation.

Before I could step over to talk to Randy, he was approached by a sophomore, a business and philosophy major, if I recall correctly. This student had a smirk on his face and came on pretty strong with Randy, trying to shake him up with a rude attitude and some foul language. Randy just smiled and asked him about his major and looked at the guy with his very loving personality. The student was taken aback by an encounter with a man who had no defense mechanisms and only kindness in his heart. The student slowly began to admit that he had tried Christianity but that it "didn't work" for him, and so deciding that it was bogus, he now made it a habit of confronting religious people on campus to debunk their beliefs. Randy smiled and looked intently at the guy and said, "Oh, that's interesting. We're actually on campus today to talk to students like you." Inexplicably, the guy seemed to melt, going from snide to sincere in just moments.

There's really no other way to explain this when it happens other than the mystery of grace, the power of the Holy Spirit working and moving through the baptized. The love of Christ was revealed simply in being close to Randy, and it very quickly brought this young man from an attack stance to a kind of real humility and vulnerability. Randy made no effort to try to convince him of anything, not even that God or that he himself loved the guy. Randy is simply convinced in his own soul that Jesus loves him, and because of this, he allows Christ to love others through him. In this case, the kid did not convert on the spot, but he began to make a sort of confession of his sins to Randy and me. While saying that he desired to be able to see how the Bible squares with science, he admitted that his doubts about religion had trapped him in a lust-filled life and a deep sadness and emptiness. Randy didn't try to convert him. I followed Randy's lead, and we encouraged him to simply seek the truth, saying that the "truth will set you free" (John 8:32). That young student walked away with hope in his eyes and in his heart.

Why did this happen? *Because there is nothing more practical in the work of evangelization than to contemplate the face of Christ.* It is no secret to anyone who has lived with Randy that his great love is prayer before the Blessed Sacrament. Everyone knows that he spends hours and hours each week in conversation with Jesus, contemplating him in his heart, loving Jesus and letting himself be loved by the Lord. We are all evangelized by Randy, and that's because the grace of his baptism has more deeply penetrated his life and personality. This does not happen without long hours spent before Jesus in prayer. St. Peter speaks of Christians as "living stones" (1 Peter 2:5). Both Randy and Rami, through their dedication to contemplating the face of Christ in the Eucharist, live in this world like a walking monstrance.

The Divine Romance

All of the talks that we give in preparation for the mission trips have become a kind of oral tradition in the seminary, and the subject of this chapter is the very first talk that we give. There is no one better at giving this talk than Thomas Gallagher, not only because he is a gifted speaker, but much more so because he lives what he says. If I can say that I am the founder of the New Evangelization Club at the seminary, Thomas Gallagher could equally make this claim. I consider it a great compliment that many people in our seminary and elsewhere mistake me for him. Thomas has the gifts of both Randy and Rami; he is a man in love with the Eucharist and can convince you that you should be too.

Thomas always begins his talk by speaking of the Samaritan woman at the well (John 4) and the way in which Jesus looked at her. Jesus revealed a "purified eros," Thomas says, a divine romance in which God comes in the flesh pursuing a soul. The Incarnation is, in Thomas' mind, the last and most loving step in the Lover's wooing of his beloved. Contemplating the face of Christ is how incarnational evangelization works. It must begin by allowing Jesus to look at us with that same love, then by coming to believe that we are the ones he seems to see, and finally by being able to look at souls with the eyes of Christ. "You need to fall in love with their souls," says Thomas. Thomas is a man's man, not a sensitive, emotional fellow prone to cry at the drop of a hat, but he is convinced that evangelization can only happen when we experience ourselves as the pursued of Jesus, who is in love with us. Only then can we pursue with the longing and eloquence of the Lover himself.

The Samaritan woman and the gaze of love that is Christ's is a good starting point. It was not an accident that Jesus wanted to stay at the well. Jesus didn't send the disciples to town to get food because he was tired of walking or out of fear of the conflict that often happened between Jews and Samaritans. Jesus is a lover seeking his beloved.

Now, I know that the Gospel says that Jesus rested by Jacob's well because he was tired from the journey, but if he was tired, it was most likely because he had spent the night before in conversation with the Father about this very broken Samaritan woman. Or perhaps he was tired because he had walked so much faster than the disciples; he didn't want to miss his opportunity to win over this woman whom he loved so much. "It was about noon," says the Gospel (John 4:6), which is not the time of day that women would go to get water. It was very hot and uncomfortable, and lugging a large water jar is not an easy thing to do in such heat. This is a signal to us that this woman was ashamed to be seen by anyone, and it becomes clear why when Jesus reveals that she is a woman of multiple divorces. The disciples are scandalized by this interaction of Jesus with a woman, especially one of such repute. We cannot be scandalized by the "pure eros" of our Lord. If we are going to learn to be evangelists, we have to enter into the divine romance of Jesus for souls of every past.

Jesus had a unique thirst just for her, and though she had had many lovers, the love of this man infinitely surpassed what was possible for a mere man. This woman experienced Jesus' love so profoundly that she forgot why she was there. She also forgot the shame that had bound her to come in the heat of the day for water. One conversation with Jesus, one look into the eyes of Love, and it changed everything for her.

Becoming Who Jesus Sees

A few years ago, while on my thirty-day silent retreat at the Institute of Priestly Formation in Omaha, I was introduced to the wonderful baptismal spirituality of Ignatian prayer. In Baptism we receive all the merits of Christ's death and resurrection. That is all the grace we need for salvation, both justifying and sanctifying grace. Another way of saying it is that Jesus begins to live in us at the moment of our baptism, and by the indwelling of the Holy Spirit, we actually become another Christ. The problem is that often *we don't feel like another Christ*; we often don't even feel like the best version of ourselves much of the time. How are we supposed to believe that he is living in us, and because of that, we are Christ to the world?

While much of the thirty days of prayer is meant to remain a mystery, which we drink from again and again so that its impact is not diminished, there are some things that are helpful for us to know for the purpose of contemplating the face of Christ. And of course, looking at the early history of the Jesuits, it is clear that Ignatius designed the Spiritual Exercises to prepare his men to become some of the greatest evangelists of all time, not least of all his first disciple, St. Francis Xavier, patron of missions. Without doing a thirty-day silent retreat, what wisdom can we glean from Ignatius?

First, it would be good to consider entering into the Spiritual Exercises in your everyday life if there is someone trained or a program to do so in your parish or area. That being said, there is still much we can gain immediately from these few insights that I will relate. St. Ignatius was a Spaniard and lived in the sixteenth century, when Catholicism in Spain was at its height. Every aspect of the culture was imbued with the affectivity of the Gospels, and to experience the religious artwork in that day must have been almost like a real encounter with the holy men and women of the Gospels themselves. Even today, Holy Week in Spain brings out statues that vividly portray the life, death, and resurrection of Christ. These statues are not like those placed out in front of most churches, which you can walk by without a thought. These are so realistic that they seem to have movement and real affections. They evoke the affectivity at the center of our hearts where our spiritual senses, the will, intellect, imagination, and desire, all coexist and are engaged. Thus, as you look at them, they even seem to look back at you.

These same affections, as with the spiritual senses, are integral to Ignatian prayer; that's the way Ignatius planned it. Each of his meditations places you in some scene from the Gospel, and you are encouraged to use your imagination and to place yourself there. The word of God is living; the Gospels are not words of past events only. Jesus is alive now, so every word of the Scriptures is said and meant not just for those he spoke to then. Each encounter of the Gospels brings, *in the present moment,* an encounter that Jesus desires to have with you and me right now. This is certainly what St. John Paul II meant when he said that the most practical first step in evangelization is the contemplation of the face of Christ and an encounter with the living God.

The Spiritual Exercises are written in Spanish, however, and can often be mistranslated, or even if accurately translated, they can be confusing. Ignatius used very specific language and strove to articulate his points as clearly and simply as possible (which was not a Spanish virtue of his time). Rather than using poetry or even prayerful prose, he is scientific in his expression. That is because he intended the Exercises to be used as a manual for the most powerful encounter with God to which a spiritual director can lead a soul in prayer.

A passage that is often misinterpreted, or at least misunderstood and therefore missed, is number 75 in the First Week of the Spiritual Exercises. In English it reads, "Consider that God our Lord beholds me."[11] But in Spanish, it is not "*que Dios*" but "*como Dios nuestros Señor.*" The word "*que*" is "that," while "*como*" is "how." To consider that God is beholding me is powerful enough and certainly would give us pause. To consider *how* God is looking at me is something altogether more transformative.

The way my mother looked at me as a boy after an act of meanness to my brother compared to how she looked at me while singing me to sleep in my boyhood bunk bed was very different. The first look required no explanation and oftentimes no punishment. How she looked at me caused me to look at myself and see my behavior. Without a word, just in how she looked at me, I understood that she knew me as a different little boy, a good little boy who would never hit his brother. By considering her loving gaze as I drifted off to sleep, I realized, deeply in my conscious (and even in my subconscious) mind, as well as in my heart, that I was loved, that I was good, that she found me to be a true delight to her. If there is any natural goodness in me, it is because of the loving gaze of my beautiful mother.

As we contemplate the face of Christ who freed the Samaritan woman from her shame in conversation at the well of Jacob, we can be sure that it was not only the words of Christ that moved her. The Word was gazing upon her. The Word was beholding her in a way that no man had been able to do. Simply in the way that he looked at her, Jesus revealed to her that he was not judging her because of her failures. He didn't love her *despite* her sins; he didn't love her *because* of her sins; he loved her *in* her sins. This makes a huge difference. *He loved HER*, the person that she really was, the saint that he had made her to be. This doesn't mean that he overlooked her sins. His love for her moved him to destroy her sins by taking the consequences for them upon himself. The consequence of his love is that her attachment or love for her sins was destroyed without destroying her. I'm sure that she never forgot how the God-man, our Lord, beheld her that day at the well, and the more she thought about it, the more she believed in his love for her. Even when she had only first believed it, however, the Gospel says, "The woman left her water jar and went back to the town and said to the people, 'Come and see the man . . . the Messiah'" (John 4:28-29).

We, too, if we contemplate the face of Christ by learning from what St. Ignatius teaches us about contemplative prayer and if we consider *how he loves us*, will come to believe in the grace of our own baptism. Grace is not a one time event; it is constantly being poured out into our lives. But it requires cooperation on our part. The spiritual exercise of considering *how* he looks at us helps us to more and more deeply cooperate with the grace of our baptism. And through this, Jesus transforms us into the person he created us to be.

Radiating Christ

A great book that is worth reading as you consider the universal vocation to evangelize as a Catholic is *Radiating Christ* by Raoul Plus, SJ.[12] The title alone says it all, and if you open up to the introduction, Fr. Plus writes, "To be a 'Christ' is the whole meaning of Christianity. To radiate Christ is the whole meaning of the Christian apostolate." It is important for us to be reminded that we are not inventing something new here. The tradition of the Church on evangelization is that it starts with contemplating the face of Christ, because the whole of the work of revealing him in our particular missions is to radiate Christ.

Fr. Raoul Plus lays out four results of the contemplation of Christ: humility, incarnational apostleship, witness of sanctity, and faith. Each of these virtues is simply the participation in the life of Christ inasmuch as he "descended from heaven," "was incarnate," "suffered," and "died" for the salvation of souls.

St. Teresa of Calcutta knew about this "thirst" for souls. She put these words in every Missionary of Charity chapel throughout the world: "I Thirst." These were Jesus' words from the cross, and Mother Teresa in her contemplation of the suffering Christ experienced that spiritual thirst in the form of a deep desolation for nearly fifty years. While no longer feeling the presence or love of God in her own heart, she never ceased to experience the love of Christ for every soul she met. This experience of love for souls, which actually increased as the years went by, was "superactualized" in her, meaning that she did nothing that was not submerged in this thirst for souls.

Mother Teresa was known for her beauty—which, if you think about it from a completely carnal standpoint, is crazy. Her face was even in the early years of her fame covered in wrinkles; she walked bent over and was never seen without a veil covering most over her head. Nevertheless, in the words of Fr. Raoul Plus, she "radiates Christ." It is not a natural thing; it is supernatural. It is not something that we can produce in ourselves; it is the love of God glowing and shining through our personalities that he himself created. That is why there are countless testimonies of those who, having met St. Mother Teresa, said that they never felt more loved in their lives than in just the few moments in her presence.

There is an amazing story, perhaps a legend, of that poor man and evangelist St. Francis of Assisi. Sitting on a donkey en route to a town, Francis went into ecstasy as he was contemplating the Lord Jesus. He was going there to preach repentance and move the people of the town to believe again in the Catholic faith, to believe in Jesus Christ. As he approached the town, he was still wrapped so deeply in prayer that he had no awareness of space and time; the love of God had overwhelmed him. The donkey, just a dumb animal, simply kept going in the direction the saint had aimed him. Even though Francis made no introductions, the people were inexplicably drawn to him and began to walk out to him from their homes and workplaces. They were drawn to him like a night moth to a shining light. They just wanted to touch him, and those who did so were healed of disease and broken limbs but, most of all, were healed of the woundedness of sin. The whole town was converted and came to believe again in Jesus.

Well, the donkey didn't stop walking, and Francis only came out of the spiritual trance when he had gone completely through the town and was arriving at the next village. He saw a young boy there and asked if it was the town he was looking for. The boy said, "No, you just passed through that town a few miles back." Francis was very surprised and confused and turned the donkey around to head back to that town.

This is the power of evangelization, and without a confidence that it is rooted in the contemplation of Christ, you will not be able to achieve what you had hoped for. Even if you have found success with any sort of method or program of evangelization, I urge you (as the Church does) to get back to prayerful consideration of the face of Christ in the Gospels. If you have ever experienced the love of God, if you have ever been amazed with the words or the stories of the holy Gospels, I encourage you to head back to that town where you first met him. Cast yourself deep into the waters of your baptism and see how he looks upon you. And even when you do get that nudge to go out and proclaim the Good News, don't let your heart move away from the place where you are confident that he loves you, and is loving others in and through you, as his living monstrance.

CHAPTER 4

How to Win Friends for Christ: Initiating Evangelizing Conversations

U p until this point, you might be thinking that there has not been much by way of practical tools to help you in the serious work of evangelization. In this chapter, we are going to get practical. We are going to show you how to start up conversations and how to take those conversations in a spiritual direction and even lead someone to a conversion of heart.

If someone had told me that this was possible before having seen it myself, I would have thought that it was a ridiculous claim—only God can convert a soul! This is true, and like we have said repeatedly, your contemplation of the face of Christ and your level of cooperation with grace and a life of virtue are major contributing factors in God's work of converting people to him. The reality of your baptism trumps any temptation or excuse inclining you to say, "It's just not my personality" or "It's not my style" or "I think it's God's job to convert people; I'm just supposed to be a good Catholic." The reality is that if you were baptized, then your personality is meant to be more and more Christlike. If you are a Catholic, then your "style" of living must in every way be conformed to this reawakening of the evangelical nature to which the Church is calling us; every conversation in some sense must be aimed at proclaiming the gospel. And if you are really living a good Catholic life, then your witness has probably already brought you many opportunities to take people by the heart and bring them into the mystery of the good news of salvation!

So I hope by now that you are beginning to discover the heart of Jesus and his thirst for the salvation of souls. In this chapter, we want to change your style and show you how just being a good Catholic will help you to make friends for Christ and influence them to become more and more open to him. St. Francis de Sales said that you can catch more flies with a spoonful of honey than with a hundred barrels of vinegar. Jesus' commandment to "make disciples of all nations" at the end of the Gospel of Matthew was prefaced by his command at the beginning of the Gospel, in the Sermon on the Mount, to "love your enemies" (Matthew 5:44; 28:19).

It is for this reason that I believe that the most practical step in preparing to evangelize is the prayer by which we come to discover the grace of our baptism. That grace means that the Holy Spirit dwells in us as the temple of God, and while we remain in a state of grace, we have charity, the very love of God, moving in us to love him and to love others—even our enemies. Knowing this, believing this, participating in his life of love from the inside out is the most vital aspect of evangelization. So when you love, what does it look like? How do we express the love that is our interior disposition? Developing the loving personality that is ours in Christ is the most practical approach because it is what we need to learn if we are going to make the love that is within us a powerful instrument for the conversion in the world.

Learning from Dale Carnegie

In what is popularly called the first "self-help" book, Dale Carnegie explains the secrets of *How to Win Friends and Influence People*.[13] If you just went by the title of the book, you might be inclined to think that this is a selfish thing; after all, "winning" friends and "influencing" people do not seem very altruistic. If you read the book, however, it becomes increasingly clear to you as a Christian that Carnegie is teaching the art of love and healthy relationships. It's not about succeeding and moving up in the world, becoming more popular or more important—though you could use these principles for that end. But if it's done out of heartfelt love, then even if it does benefit you, it benefits you because love is an end in itself. The most effective way to live is always to love. History bears out that those who hold material success as a higher end than God and union with him in Christ hijack the techniques of love. For a time, they may appear to be more successful; but ultimately. those people are found out, and their edifice of insincerity is toppled down.

The difference between an evangelist and a proselytizer is that the second has the goal of convincing you to believe because in some sense, he or she thinks you are not lovable to God unless you believe and obey that doctrine. Proselytizers are often experts at arguing. But evangelists love you before they know you; they love you, and they believe that God loves you because you are an unrepeatable good for whom the only response is love. They do not believe that God loves you *despite* your sins; they believe that God loves you *in* your sins, because God loves you—for your own sake. An evangelist hopes that you come to know God's love for you and that you begin or grow in a relationship with him through Jesus in the power of the Holy Spirit. An evangelist believes that he or she is cooperating with God's will and love for you by loving you with his love. It is the Holy Spirit working within the evangelist through incarnational charity.

How Do You Love?

Obviously, there are quite a few books that we recommend reading, praying with, and applying to the lives of evangelizers. In our training, we have "baptized" Dale Carnegie's book and changed the title to this: "How to Win Friends and Influence People for Christ." This chapter will be helpful for you, but it is advisable to do a serious reading of his book, as it is one of the most practical guides in learning how to love. I have spent a great deal of time praying with and thinking about the wisdom of St. Francis de Sales in his classic work *Introduction to the Devout Life*, and you can seriously grow in virtue and prayer from reading it. But if you read Dale Carnegie's book and make a habit of his principles, you will exteriorly appear to be as loving a person as St. Francis de Sales hoped to make you. Dale Carnegie does not have the wisdom or insight of St. Francis regarding interior transformation, but I know many people who have read and prayed with the *Introduction of the Devout Life* whom I wish would also read Dale Carnegie.

Because St. Paul's words are read at so many weddings, we can tend to shut down when we hear, "Love is patient; love is kind; it holds no record of wrongs it does not envy; it does not boast; love never despairs" (cf. 1 Corinthians 13:4-7). But even though we have heard it repeatedly, we can often find ourselves going to Confession again and again, saying that we have failed in patience, failed to be kind, failed to forgive, or were jealous and proud. We confess these things because we feel sorry for having done them and desire not to do them again. We also fail to succeed in charity because we have not perhaps ever been trained in how to love. What is love, anyway?

A simple definition of love is "to will the good for another." Jesus gives in John 15 a new commandment of love: "Love one another as I love you. . . . Lay down [your] life for [your] friends" (verses 12, 13). As we mentioned above, he also says that we must love our enemies, and even love them as we love ourselves. This is hard, so he also says, "The person who is trustworthy in very small matters is also trustworthy in great ones" (Luke 16:10). Dale Carnegie's principles are those small matters, which if we supplement them with the interior virtue for which De Sales is the foremost guide, we will be able to love in the most challenging circumstances—laying down our lives for our friends and even loving our enemies as ourselves.

Simple Suggestions for Showing Interest and Love

As we said earlier in the chapter on prayer, evangelization begins well before you meet a person—*you need to be praying for them*. This interior disposition, we have found, can be very practical. What I suggest in order to bring that prayer into conversations is to look at each person you meet and *say in your heart, "I love you" or "God loves you."* If you do this for several consecutive days, you will begin to actually think it before you say it and also feel it when you say it.

Some years back, while I was an undergraduate, there was an annoying student who greeted me with an insult—although in jest—every time I saw him. After a few weeks of this, I realized that I was walking the long way to the cafeteria to avoid him. I decided that I needed to pray for and about him because he was driving me crazy. In prayer I realized that he actually was hoping that I would want to become his friend, but he didn't know how, other than to make fun of me. It occurred to me that it would have been amazingly powerful if instead of calling me a stupid name, he were to give me a "high-five" and say, "You're the man!" I tried to tell him this, but he didn't catch on—he still used the insulting greeting. Nevertheless, I took my own advice and starting greeting people that way, and I found it to be tremendously effective. Though naturally shy, I woke up a few months later and discovered that I knew half the students on campus. It would have been even more powerful if I had also been able to look at each person and say in my heart, "God loves you."

Doing this is a highly effective way for starting up conversations. On our first mission trip, one seminarian just stood in the center of the quad saying hello to people while in his heart trying to imagine how much Jesus loves each one of the students. A reporter from the campus walked up to him and talked to him for a good while, asking him what we were all about and wanting to do a story on us for the school paper. He snapped the seminarian's photo and said, "You have a very welcoming face; I'm going to use your photo for this article. I wish all religious people were as pleasant as you all are." Little did the reporter know that that seminarian was extremely shy and had never done any sort of evangelization in his entire life.

Here are some other suggestions to help you start evangelizing conversations:

• *Smiling* is part of love's power. For some of us, it takes great effort to smile. I am always self-conscious when I smile—I'm not sure why. Something happens when you smile though, both to your own brain and to the person to whom your smile is directed. For you, it actually sends signals to your brain telling you that you are happy. So even if you are extremely nervous about talking to strangers or about the faith, you will actually be fighting those temptations through the act of smiling—and if you don't give up, you will overcome your anxieties. If you don't smile and you are nervous, your brain will send signals to your face that will show to whomever you are speaking that you are nervous and/or frightened, and they might misperceive your facial expression and think you are actually angry.

Working hard at a smile even if you don't like to smile or feel happier as a result is, however, just a loving thing to do and is very effective. It puts people at ease. They see you smile, and just like the contagiousness of a yawn, their reaction is to smile back, and interiorly they suddenly feel a bit happier. They also are choosing to receive and give back to you what you have given, which is another way to define love: giving and receiving. Starting up the conversation will be much easier if you begin with a smile.

• *Eye contact* is as important as smiling. Eye contact tells the person that you are truly interested. Jesus, "looking at him, loved him" (Mark 10:21). You might be saying in your heart, "I love this person." You might be smiling and even saying words that would otherwise indicate a true interest in that person. But if you are looking at the ground or off into the distance or at their face and not into their eyes, your lack of eye contact tells them that you are not interested and that you might be smiling about something else and not at them. Perhaps the rich young man whom Jesus looked upon and loved looked down just before Jesus gazed upon him with his sanctifying eyes. Jesus wants to look with love through *your* eyes.

• *Handshake.* While it might not always be prudent or necessary to extend a hand in your greeting, if you do, don't do the floppy handshake nor the overpowering strong-arm handshake. On a college campus, some people will not want to shake your hand, some will give you a fancy high-five, and some will want to give you a hug before you even know their names. You just have to roll with every reaction. As you shake a person's hand, reflect on how Jesus embraced those he encountered. "He took the child by the hand and said to her, '*Talitha koum*,'" (Mark 5:41). When Simon Peter began to sink in the water, Jesus "stretched out his hand and caught him," helping him into the boat (Matthew 14:31). When the leper said to Jesus, "Lord, if you wish, you can make me clean," Jesus "stretched out his hand, touched him, and said, 'I will do it. Be made clean'" (Matthew 8:2, 3).

• *Posture.* Your posture is crucial as well. If you turn with your shoulders squarely toward people but lean in, they will feel a bit intimidated, and you may come across as overbearing. If you turn your body sideways away from them, they may feel that you are not very interested in them. But if you remain relaxed, standing with humble confidence with one hand at your side, shoulders almost squarely toward them (we usually have a Bible or a handful of fliers in the other hand), then you will come across in a more pleasing manner. Don't stand too close, but don't be afraid of close talkers—bear with them even if it makes you uncomfortable.

When thinking about how to approach other people in conversation, it's helpful to keep in mind the posture of Jesus who, though God, humbled himself, becoming a servant. Based on the Shroud of Turin, Jesus was probably about a head taller than the average man of his day. We cannot say for the most part how or where he stood, but if he were tall, he would certainly have had to lower himself to enter every house. And when he spoke to the woman caught in adultery, he went all the way to the ground, probably both as an act of humility and also to take the focus off of her who was in such a shameful state (John 8:1-11).

• *Show a true interest in the person.* Of all the recommendations of Dale Carnegie, this is the most significant. To take a true interest in a person is to love them, to desire their good. St. Francis de Sales, in his classic *Introduction to the Devout Life*, wrote,

> In so far as divine love enriches us it is called grace, which makes us pleasing to God. In so far as it gives us the strength to do good, it is called charity. But when it grows to such a degree of perfection that it makes us not only to do good but rather moves us to do it carefully, frequently and promptly, it is called devotion. . . . In short, devotion is nothing else than a spiritual agility and liveliness by means of which charity realizes its actions in us, or we do so by charity, promptly and lovingly.[14]

The difference between loving someone and liking someone can be compared to the difference between charity and devotion. In the first case, you are doing your duty; there is a basic respect for their goodness and likeness to God. In the second case, you are contemplating the face of Christ in that person, and so you can begin to delight in both their best qualities and also in their quirks. And the reason this is so important for evangelization is because if you are merely being charitable to a person, that person will know it, and if you really like the person and are delighting in him, he will also know it. And by doing this, according to Dale Carnegie, the person begins to like you and even delight in you. Unconditional love means that you love someone with both his graceful and ungraceful qualities. To delight in a person—that is the way that Jesus wants us to love people, most of all sinners, backsliders, those rejected by the world, and even those who hate us.

• *Listen, listen, listen!* Be extraordinarily patient with people. You are not a lawyer or even an apologist. You are fulfilling your vocation to evangelize, to be Jesus to someone else. Think of how Jesus listens to you when you pray. We get distracted and go off on so many tangents with God in prayer—but he never stops listening to us. By doing this, he allows us to listen to ourselves and see our many wrongheaded ways of thinking and living. By listening, you make space for people to encounter God, just as the Holy Spirit makes space in our own prayer to encounter the Father and the Son. As you listen to someone, realize that you are listening to him or her in the place of Jesus. So be extremely attentive to what people say; repeat back to them what you have understood them to mean. Ask for clarifications only to show that you hear them and respect them, not so much to challenge their view.

While I was in Ethiopia, I didn't speak the language at all. I would smile at the people we approached. I would look them in the eye, and I could say enough to ask them, "Tell me your story." I was just trying to love them as they spoke to me. Then I would turn to the translator to hear what they had said, and he would tell me, "They said that you're such an amazing listener. You're such a loving person." And all that I was doing was sitting there and smiling at them!

The Rule of Politeness

There is an unwritten rule of polite conversation in our country that goes something like this: *if you listen to me for five minutes, then I owe two to three minutes of listening to you.* This is different for each person; for some, five minutes of listening gets you one minute to speak, and for others, it is five minutes for five minutes. Regardless, this is a reality that is very helpful for conversations about faith. It also means that as much as possible, you have to stay on a similar or compatible topic. So if you listen to a person talk about a personal view, you can't change the subject to a personal view of your own that is completely unrelated to what the person has spoken about. But if you stay on their topic, even if your view is opposite to theirs (as long as you are not directly attacking their view), then they will feel obliged to listen to you for at least one-fifth of the time that you have listened to them. In other words, get them to talk and enjoy who they are and what they say or at least how they say it, and in a sense, they will *have to listen* to you.

For one seminarian, it seemed as if perhaps evangelizing would not be his strong suit, but he had completed the training and went out with us and tried it. He and his teammate got split up, and he, being a smoker, decided that he would do best by talking to other smokers. All day long he smoked cigarette after cigarette, asking open-ended questions to men and women at the smoking gazebo. I saw him there by himself for a good while and wanted to make sure that he was okay without his teammate. To be discrete, I walked up slowly and was blessed to hear the end of a conversation. He had listened to a student for two to three full cigarettes, which in smoker's language adds up to about twenty-five to thirty-five minutes. She would smoke her cigarette, and he would listen for the whole cigarette and just smile and nod. Once finished, he would respond, "Well, that's an interesting perspective. I've never heard it said quite like that before. What if we looked at it this way?" He would quickly complete his statement, which showed no condemnation of her view or her dignity. His were one-minute responses to her seven- to ten-minute statements. She would then respond to his spin on the topic and light up another cigarette and go on for another seven to ten minutes, and his only response was active listening: "Oh, how about that! (smile, nod); oh, yes, indeed . . . " Saying very little for the first thirty minutes, each time he nudged the conversation a little more toward religion. She finally asked, "Well, I'm actually very interested; now what is it that you believe?"

He then gave a simple but logical explanation of the Catholic faith, connecting it to those things she had said and to what he knew about her up to that point. I could barely believe my ears when I heard her respond with a detached determination, "Well, I'm quite sure that you're right about that. It's really just a matter of time before I become a Catholic, I guess."

"What do you mean exactly, 'a matter of time'?" I chimed in, a bit more excited than I should have let on. "Oh," she replied, "just because I'm a full-time student and work full-time. But in a year or so after I graduate, I'm going to go through the process and become a Catholic; I mean, it's clearly the Church that Jesus founded, [as the seminarian had said], and happiness can only come through knowing Jesus in the sacraments." Perhaps she never took that step of becoming Catholic, just like many cigarette smokers who know that cigarettes cause lung cancer but don't quit smoking. Nevertheless, she was convinced that Catholicism was the key to her happiness and was the Church founded by Christ. Grace was clearly at work, but this seminarian had loved her very well by his use of the "rule of politeness."

This same rule works in another way, like a monetary exchange. You give someone twenty minutes to speak, maybe right before that person has to leave. Then, instead of just going right into the long response, you say, "Hey, look, I can see you need to go, and I know that you and I may not be able to talk again about this. So I have one thing to say to you, a bit off the topic, but I feel I'd be doing you an injustice if I do not say this, *and* it will only take three minutes." They will actually feel as if you are giving them a really good deal—even though in terms of cash in hand, you are giving them nothing.

This leads us into the basic rules of kerygma, the proclaiming of the gospel, and our next chapter. But first, below are some tips for evangelizing conversations.

The "Dos and Don'ts" of Evangelizing Conversations

When we train missionaries at the Mount, we give them a list of conversational "dos and don'ts" as a quick reference.

- Don't criticize, condemn, or complain.
- Fulfill another person's desire to feel important.
- You cannot influence people by telling them what they want to hear.
- You can make more friends in two months by becoming interested in other people than you can in two years by trying to get other people interested in you.
- Smile.
- The most beautiful sound in the world to people is the sound of their own name.
- To become an excellent conversationalist, talk less and listen more.
- Interest people by talking about the subject in which they are most interested.
- To get people to like you, say something complimentary.
- You can't win an argument, so don't get into arguments.
- You can't change a person's mind by logic or anger.
- You *can* change another person's mind by talking about your faults. This is disarming to people and disposes them to the humility it takes to be not only open to another view but even to agree with it and change the way they live.
- Admit when you are wrong.
- To influence people, show that you really believe in the image of themselves that they present to you.
- Never presume the worst, and trust what people tell you.
- Find out the reason behind someone's action, which will help make you more empathetic.

- If you want attention, use the power of dramatization to make the gospel sound like the amazing thing that it should be.
- If you have something unpleasant to say, first say something nice.
- Never nag or embarrass another person in front of their friends or family.
- Never criticize your evangelization partner.
- Give honest appreciation.
- Be as excited to meet someone as when you see your favorite person.
- Use all of these techniques out of heartfelt love and sincerity.

In addition, in our training we tell the missionaries that if someone says something that we know is wrong or incorrect, we let them know about it indirectly. We don't want to embarrass the person we are talking to—we are evangelists, not lawyers, and we don't want to trap that person in a corner.

We never give direct orders, but if nothing else works, assertive communication can be a last step in the process. The missionary can say, "This is my challenge to you. I dare you to read the Gospels for yourself and then state in prayer or publicly that you don't believe in Jesus." Of course, we want to do all these things in love. We want to praise any progress we detect, and we want to emphasize a person's strengths so that they use their strengths to build up their weaknesses.

CHAPTER 5

Proclaiming the Kerygma: The Essential Gospel Message

The first day we were on campus for our first mission trip, I was in several long conversations with students, one after another until about one in the afternoon—that is to say, without a break. I really had to use the bathroom, but as I was walking into the building deliriously rushing to the toilet, the Holy Spirit gave me such a strong nudge to go and speak with a particular young man that I almost postponed my trip. "Lord, I'll be right back," I promised. While washing my hands, an overwhelming temptation came over me to avoid talking to this guy; I also experienced feelings of inferiority, sadness, and shame. While this temptation continued, I decided to walk back out and approach the student. He was a very big fellow—he had obviously played football or was perhaps considering a job as a professional wrestler. This large guy was standing with a friend, smoking a cigarette quickly, as if on a study break or on his way to his next class. I again was filled with a temptation to refrain from talking to him.

"How's it going, brother?" I asked with half a smile and nod of the head. His voice was deep but showed surprise as I approached him.

"Chillin', my man," he said.

"Nice weather for February, eh?"

"Yeah, this is the first nice day we've had for a good long while," he replied and added, "Hey, I've seen all you priests around here all day. What are you all up to on our campus anyway?"

"We're just out spreading the good; you know what I mean?"

"Right on, brother, right on; I like that. So you all just talk to students, having a good time and all this, then, eh?"

"Basically, yeah, that's about it." I could tell he was more disposed to talk than some others, and now I understood why those temptations not to talk to him had come to me so strongly. He also seemed as if he had to get going, but I didn't want to rush into anything, so I asked, "So what do you study here?"

"I'm business and economics."

"What year?" I asked.

"Sophomore—I hope to graduate on time, though." (I guess that's not so common these days.)

"Good man," I replied. "So you must like what you study."

"You got to do the work if you want to eat," he said, and I wondered if he was not as much of an academic as just a good guy with natural virtue to do his best in work and school. "I used to not like school, but now I got these loans and want to do well for myself, and so I keep a tight schedule."

"It looks like you like to lift weights too," I said.

"Yeah, yeah, I do, got to! It's the only thing that keeps me sane with school and work." I must confess that, even once the temptations were gone, I was still intimidated by this very large and capable fellow.

"So like I said, I'm out here to spread the good, and I've been listening to you speak and am very impressed with you, bro—and not just with your enormous arms." He smiled and chuckled. "I have a more serious question for you, though. What's your faith background? And what do you believe?"

"Well, I guess I don't really have one, you know? I mean, my mom and me and my siblings, we don't really have any religion. But I think my dad was Catholic or something."

"Did he ever take you to church or anything?" I asked him.

"No, well, maybe once or twice when we were kids."

"Okay, well, what do you think about religion, or Catholicism, rather?"

"It's okay, I guess. Well, I don't even really know; nobody's ever told me anything about it, so what can I say, I don't even know."

"So nobody ever told you how to have a relationship with God through Jesus Christ?"

"No, never," he said.

"Well, have you ever looked into it yourself, to see what Jesus himself said about how to have a relationship with him?"

"No, nothing, bro. I don't really know anything." Here is when you know that you are about to see the miracle of conversion. He's never heard anything, bad or good, yet he's a pretty good guy, at least shows some natural virtue, and he's not at all put off by these kinds of questions.

"Would you like me to show you real quickly the words of Jesus about what a relationship with him means?"

"Yes, absolutely I would," he responded. So I opened up the Bible that I had to this passage, John 14:15-21, and invited him to read it to himself quietly:

"If you love me, you will keep my commandments. And I will ask the Father, and he will give you another Advocate to be with you always, the Spirit of truth, which the world cannot accept, because it neither sees nor knows it. But you know it, because it remains with you, and will be in you. I will not leave you orphans; I will come to you. In a little while the world will no longer see me, but you will see me, because I live and you will live. On that day you will realize that I am in my Father and you are in me and I in you. Whoever has my commandments and observes them is the one who loves me. And whoever loves me will be loved by my Father, and I will love him and reveal myself to him."

It's only a few verses, but it took him what felt like five to ten minutes to finish reading it, and I watched as tears began to well up in his eyes.

Finally, he put the little Bible down from his eyes, and I said, "Pretty powerful words, eh?" He couldn't speak; he knew that if he did, he would begin to cry, and though his friend had stood there quietly the whole time, he was probably more aware of him than I was. So I asked, "Would you like to say a prayer with me right now, asking to begin a relationship with God through Jesus Christ?" He nodded and put his head down as he said, "Absolutely, I would."

I then pulled out the little cards we carry to give to people who say yes to this question, and I gave one to him, one to his friend, and I kept one and said, "Let's pray this out loud together." It reads, "Jesus, come into my life. Reveal yourself to me. Free me from my sins and lead me to the truth. Reveal to me your mercy in the power of your resurrection. Lord Jesus Christ, prove to me your love and lead me to everlasting life." His head was down and his shoulders relaxed forward, with his hands together. I don't remember what I said at that point, but he came in for a hug, and this big impressive man broke down in tears there in the center of the GMU campus. I told him how much God loves him and that it was God's love that he was experiencing in that moment.

As he finished crying, I told him to turn the card over and read it because it explains clearly that this prayer is only the beginning of a relationship with Christ and that to establish the fullness of that friendship with God (as St. Thomas Aquinas puts it), he would need to be baptized and become a fully initiated Catholic. He read this and asked, "How do I do this?"

"Well, truth be told, we are only here for a few days, but I can certainly talk to you more while I'm here." I turned to the guy who had quietly stood there beside us and asked, "Hey, what's your deal? Are you Catholic?"

"Yeah." He paused and I said, "Well, you've got a serious task on your hands. It's your job to get . . . " and I then paused as I realized in embarrassment that I had not asked for their names. Turning to the big guy, I asked, "Wait. What's your name, my brother?"

He smiled and said, "Mike; they call me Big Mike."

"And what's your name, my Catholic brother?" The somewhat shy guy said, "I'm Mike too, actually."

"Okay, Mike and Big Mike, you're in an excellent place and have an exciting journey ahead of you. Big Mike, Mike is going to help you go through the process of becoming Catholic and continuing to grow in your relationship with God in Jesus Christ." I then grabbed Mike's sleeve and looked him in the eyes and said, "Do you understand how serious this is? You've just watched your friend go through a serious conversion, so you have to make sure he's able to see it through. It is Ash Wednesday in two days; the campus ministry chapel is just a few blocks away. I will see you there on Wednesday night and introduce you to the priest."

"Oh, I know Fr. Peter already."

"Great," I said. "Well, then bring Big Mike and bring another friend, and Ill see you there."

They were already late for a class, so I ended quickly; otherwise, I would have gotten their cell phone numbers and made sure of all this myself. I saw Big Mike the next day in the cafeteria and talked to him more about Jesus and gave him a Bible and more information on the campus ministry. I also found out that he was *the* cool kid on campus and literally everyone knew him, so I had him introduce me to some of his other friends there. He was looking a bit ill that day, however, and on Ash Wednesday he did not show up—but the other Mike did, and he brought Big Mike's buddy, one of the leaders of their fraternity (we'll call him John).

John walked right up to Fr. Peter and said, "Fr. Peter, I'm Catholic and a junior here at GMU, but I've not been coming to Mass, and I ask your forgiveness and now promise to you that I will start coming from now on." I asked Mike about Big Mike and apparently he had gotten much sicker and had to go home, but he was very sorry he was unable to come, and both were still committed to the Lord and to the plan.

The Gospel, the Power of God

This story tells us a great deal about how powerfully God can work through any of us. But for now, just focusing on the kerygma itself, notice that I did very little. I mostly asked questions and I listened; I didn't even state in my own words or out loud the words of proclamation. Nevertheless, the gospel "is the power of God for the salvation of everyone who believes. . . . For in it is revealed the righteousness of God" (Romans 1:16, 17). When the gospel is read or simply stated or proclaimed through powerful declarations, power flows from God through whichever instrument God uses, man or book, and enters into the soul of the hearer or reader. Faith is given (as seen in the converts on Pentecost), the faith of those who already believe is awakened, and faith's power is manifested in miracles and conversions. And though man must cooperate with this, it is God who is working through his instruments.

The normative means of coming to faith is not, in fact, infant baptism. The normative means of coming to faith is through hearing the gospel, proclaimed by a Catholic who is fulfilling his or her duty to share the gospel. This might seem backwards to the Catholic mind-set. We are used to seeing only infants baptized and only hearing a priest proclaim the gospel, and only in church. Did I say only in church? What a pity it is that there are so many Catholics who do not know what the gospel is or how to share it with others! There is a spiritual poverty in our world, a famished hunger for God, and we have him. Yet even many priests have little clue as to how to share this hidden treasure—the kerygma, the proclamation of the gospel!

In the story above, you read what I think is the easiest way to share the kerygma: let the Gospels do all the work. Two simple questions lead into it. First: *Has anyone ever shown you how to have a relationship with Jesus Christ?* Second: *Have you ever read for yourself what Jesus himself says about how to have a relationship with God?*

Next, you simply have to have one of those passages from the New Testament that speaks of the intimacy that God wants to have with us. John 14:15-21 is good because it shows how much God desires to dwell within us. It also shows that we have to say yes to him and that the commandments are not a list of rules but our response of love to a God who loves us first and loves us so much more than we could ever love him.

You then let the person read it; don't make him read it out loud unless you know he is a good reader. Ask the person to read it to himself and to take his time and really think about the meaning of the words. If he or she really does what you ask, a kind of *lectio divina,* or sacred reading, happens. Many people, even if they have heard the gospel before, will have some kind of an experience of consolation or sense of God's presence. The word will open them, disposing them to God and to what you have to say to them.

I have asked well over one thousand people the two questions above—Catholics, Protestants, and non-Christians. Even among Protestants, there are quite a few who answer no to both questions. So far, only a handful of Catholics have answered these questions in the positive, and most of those who said yes, when questioned further, only knew "the rules" of Catholicism, and even about those, they were often unclear.

Now, there are a good number of Catholics who have a relationship with God, but they simply have never heard it spoken of in that way or at all. This includes the large percentage of Catholics who rarely come to church. Even if they do come, they don't find the parish or the campus ministry to be a place where they hear a lot of people talking about Jesus or the gospel or faith or where they meet people who want to pray or grow in their relationship with God together. It is these people to whom I've asked these questions, and they say, far too many times, "No, never; I have never heard a priest, catechist, or one of my parents ever show me the words of Jesus in the gospel explaining how to have a relationship with him." If they do come to a relationship with the Lord, they may be angry for a time because no one ever shared it with them before. But once they do have such a relationship, joy outweighs any pain or loss of time from not knowing the intimacy of God.

The gospel is the seed of salvation. Unless it spreads, it will not be able to sink into the soil of human hearts, to be watered by grace, to be tilled by the love of brothers and sisters in faith, or to sprout into eternal life. Surely if we scatter this seed, there will be seeds that fall upon the rock, on the path, and into the thorns. Yet still it must be said, "Woe to us if we do not proclaim the gospel" (cf. 1 Corinthians 9:16), because there are many Catholic hearts that have been tilled and watered and that would be ready to sprout—but the gospel has not yet been planted.

Proclaim the Good News Out Loud

The easy way—having people read from the Bible themselves—is much more effective for producing the good fruit you hope to bear. But for some reason, Jesus asks us to *proclaim* the good news! (Matthew 28:19). That is, to state it out loud to another person so that they can hear and believe it—usually with the intention of them coming to believe it, although not necessarily.

A friend of mine was telling me that his son (we'll call him George), whom he had raised as a devout Protestant, had fallen away from Jesus. He was now either an agnostic or atheist. It was hard for this man to see his son walk away from the faith that he had worked so hard to instill in him, but he understood that it was not in his power to convert but only to do his best to teach and lead his son to Christ. Well, George was in his second semester of college and met another young man who was not raised in any faith. The young man (we'll call him Steve) was very interested in religion and was a great religions major. He began to ask George all kinds of questions about his faith upbringing. Apparently, Steve had not gotten to the course on Christianity yet and knew very little about it at that point. "I don't believe it anymore, so I guess it doesn't really matter what I was taught," said George.

"Please, could you at least tell me what your parents believed or what they taught you?" asked Steve.

Though hesitant because he didn't believe it himself, George explained, "Well, the basic idea is that God, the Creator of all things, made man to be in relationship with him and placed the first man and woman in a garden at the beginning of time. They rejected God, and sin and death came into the world as a result, and now Christians believe that all people have this original sin in them, which separates us from God. It's all baloney if you ask me, but anyway, God still loved us so he sent his only Son, God, in the person of Jesus Christ, who became a man and lived a normal human life. He preached and taught, and they think he did lots of miracles—I don't buy it. Then he took the sins of all humanity onto himself, and he died on a cross to take the penalty for our sins and reconcile us to God. After three days, he rose from the dead, and now he is in heaven seated at the right hand of God. What my parents believe is that if you believe in him and are baptized in his name, you will be born again and have eternal life, but if you reject him and the gospel, then you will have eternal damnation."

Immediately Steve came to believe and begged George to tell him more, to tell him everything, and as a result, George began to reconsider his faith. The Holy Spirit worked powerfully in

George's life, and he now reads and prays with the Scriptures every day and is a mighty evangelist, simply because he proclaimed the kerygma.

When we teach the seminarians, I always proclaim the gospel to them so that they can see an example of what it looks like when someone does so. So far 100 percent of the time—this is among men in formation to become Catholic priests, mind you—100 percent of the time, one of the seminarians comes up to me and we have a conversation that goes something like this:

"Ah, Thomas, can I ask you a question?"

"Sure, buddy, anything you want."

"What was that thing that you did in your talk?"

"That thing I did?"

"What did you call it? The *kariggeema?*" he asks.

I have to laugh to myself because it's probably a combination of my mispronunciation and the fact they've never heard the word before.

"Oh, the kerygma, you mean?"

"Yes, well, something happened to me when you said it, and I've never felt like this before. I feel warm and excited, and my heart is pounding."

"HA! You've been struck with the power of God, my friend! The grace of your baptism is being activated in your soul; God has been working in you without you, and you've been working in the Church without him. Now you are alive in Christ!" Perhaps that's a bit dramatic, but I want them to feel all the effects and excitement of realizing what they are experiencing—God's power, God's love! I've been asked not to tell anyone who these seminarians are because it's a fairly embarrassing thing, both for the seminarian himself and for the diocese. After all, here the diocese is forming a priest who has not yet heard or come to believe the essential gospel message: that God loves him and wants a relationship with him.

There is a big difference between obeying the commandments because it's the right thing to do versus realizing that God loves you and that you are loving him back and cooperating with the Holy Spirit within your soul. It's quite different to state intellectually that you believe the doctrines and dogmas of the Creed versus believing it in your heart and receiving God's heart into your heart in a personal relationship. This is what is lacking in so many Catholics, oftentimes because they think it's Protestant doctrine—false! It's what the Church has always believed; it's what the Scriptures were written for; it's what the Creed was fought for; it's what monasteries were built for; it's what the great evangelists proclaimed; it's what Vatican II's universal call to holiness is all about! It's what Catholicism is all about—every doctrine, every sacrament, all of it. It's about a personal relationship with God!

On the first day of the first mission trip to GMU, there was another amazing experience that ought to be shared. One of the other seminarians was uncomfortable about starting up conversations, and so I offered to join him. (I refrained from telling him that I was also incredibly nervous.) So we got some food, and since it was lunchtime, we walked up to a nearly full table and asked, "Can we join you all for lunch?" They all looked at each other, chuckled, and said, "Sure, yes, please join us." In the first five minutes, we discovered that everyone at the table was either atheist, agnostic, ex-Catholic, anti-Catholic, living a homosexual or bisexual lifestyle, or all of the above. When I realized this, I said, "I now know why you all laughed when we asked to join you for lunch. You knew that we came to the right table." Well, the rules of love and politeness held true, and after we had asked them several open-ended questions, they then asked one question after another, and for almost an hour we did our best to answer them.

One of the guys, who happened to be "all of the above," whom we will call Jack, asked us one more final question and then said, "Shoot, I have to go to class. Well, it was fun talking anyway."

"Well, we could walk with you," we offered, and he agreed. So we walked with him, and instead of answering his question, we asked him about himself. He told us the whole story of how he went from being a baptized and confirmed Catholic to becoming an active homosexual anti-Catholic atheist. It was hard to hear, but at the end we thanked him for sharing his story, and we parted ways.

The next day I ran into him again with a different seminarian, and we spoke with Jack for several hours. At the end of the conversation, without making any argument from religion, Jack agreed that we do have immaterial souls, and in some sense, this must mean that there is some sort of spiritual being that brought all things into existence and whose presence has given some sense of immateriality to us and perhaps other beings. Very vague stuff, a start, but he concluded by adding, "But it doesn't matter; all of this is just my opinion and yours. No one can really know this stuff—it's all relative."

The third day was our last day on campus. I was excited about all the conversions that we had seen and yet sad that I would not have another day there. I saw Jack at a table on the other side of the cafeteria and immediately knew that I had to speak to him. I walked over to him. He was sitting with some of his friends from the first day and also a student from campus ministry. I thanked Jack for our pleasant discussions from the past two days, and he thanked me. Then I said, "Jack, I am leaving now and have the conviction that God has one more thing for me to say to you." This was the first time that I had directly invoked God's name in this way with him.

"Okay," he said with a curious smile.

"God loves you; he's in love with you, and he longs to have a relationship with you; and on behalf of the Catholic Church, I am here to invite you to come back to the Church and reconsider the faith of your birth and the personal relationship that God desires for you." Both Jack and his friend had tears in their eyes, and he said, "That's the most amazing thing that anyone has ever said to me! Thank you, Thomas, thank you so much! I will never forget you, and I will seriously consider your offer."

Jack has gone back and forth several times since that day in regard to his faith. Unfortunately, he is still immersed in a homosexual lifestyle from which it is extremely difficult to break free. Had Catholicism been offered to him as a relationship when he was growing up, maybe he never would have left the Church. But speculation aside, he is proof, along with the hundreds of other relativists to whom we have spoken and proposed Catholicism as a personal relationship, that relativism is not overcome by logical arguments. Many are not really capable of reasonable, rational dialogue because sometimes they view even science as just opinion. To them everything is personal belief, personal view, personal preference, or personal spirituality. So all you need to do is introduce them to the Person of Jesus Christ, the personal God who became a man. Become a mediator of that relationship, that friendship with God, and they will find that Truth is as hard to resist as the irresistibly attractive incarnation of Love who, most important, loves them personally.

Below is listed the essential points that constitute the kerygma, as well as a sample kerygma in my own words. These can help you as you practice sharing the kerygma with others.

Kerygma: Essential Proclamation of the Gospel Message of Jesus Christ

Fundamental Points

- "God loves you, he's in love with you, and he longs to have a relationship with you. On behalf of the Catholic Church, I invite you to learn more about Jesus Christ and the holy Church that he founded."

- All that we believe in our faith is centered on having a relationship with God. If there is no encounter or relationship, the Church does seem like a bunch of rules and restrictions because everything is seen out of order. (Many Protestants do not know Catholics can talk this way or believe this.)
- Jesus became man, died on the cross for our sins, and rose from the dead. If you are baptized and believe in him, then you will be saved.
- The power of Christ's death and resurrection comes through hearing the gospel message.
- In making this a declaration, the Holy Spirit is given the opportunity to work in that moment in the soul and heart of the hearer to make the ascent of faith.
- Every person has a spiritual longing for a personal relationship with God. God made each person for himself.
- The kerygma will be individualized for each person and will fit the person to whom we are talking.

Essentials of the Kerygma

1. God created us for a relationship with him.
2. This relationship is broken through sin. The world was fallen until the Christ event.
3. Jesus restores our relationship with the Father. He died on the cross for every person throughout history. Jesus made it possible for that relationship and life to last forever.
4. We have the choice to accept or reject this offer of his love.

If you repent, believe in the gospel, are baptized, confirmed, and receive Holy Communion, you are initiated into that everlasting life called "covenant."

Sample Kerygma

Jesus Christ is the Son of God, fully man and fully God, the Word of God born of a human mother taking on our same humanity. Though God by his very nature, in becoming man Jesus was able to take the sin of humanity onto himself in order to redeem us from sin. He died for you, for your salvation, so that you could have a personal relationship with God.

Jesus did this by offering himself in obedience to God the Father, surrendering his life to torture and crucifixion, the capital punishment of his day. By dying on the cross, he took the penalty for our sins—yours and mine—and reunited us to God in a way that we could never do on our own. Because of our sins, there had been an unbridgeable gap between God and us. Jesus was our ransom to the Father for our salvation; he bridged the gap and did so much more for us. Those who believe in him, accepting all that he teaches, are baptized in the name of the Father and of the Son and of the Holy Spirit and are made sons and daughters of God, united to him for all eternity. Through Adam, sin came into the world, and all generations following him were born into sin. In Christ, all of humanity was redeemed, and those who accept that redemption offered by Christ on the cross are truly saved.

Saved from what? Saved from death, essentially. Because we were born into a world wounded by the sin of our first father, we all are going to die eventually. But Jesus, after offering himself up on the cross, rose from the dead after three days in the tomb. He descended to the abode of the dead and revealed his salvation there. He proclaimed to them that if they believe in him and follow him, they will rise from the dead with him at the end of time and spend an eternity with him—and with God the Father and the Holy Spirit—in a glorified body. At that time, there will be a new heaven and a new earth. Jesus rose from the dead to reveal to us what will be our lot if we believe in him.

Jesus is offering to you salvation through a personal relationship with him. This salvation/relationship can begin in you by being initiated into what Jesus calls his "new and everlasting covenant." All the grace of his death and resurrection is given through the Sacraments of Baptism, Confirmation, and the Eucharist. These are the Sacraments of Initiation into the everlasting covenant with Jesus Christ.

CHAPTER 6

Personal Testimony:
How to Share Your Story

The first conversations between the small group of seminarians that later blossomed into the mission trips began with a zeal to know and spread the gospel. Some of us had experience with FOCUS (Fellowship of Catholic University Students), which teaches how to evangelize through relationships. We knew that in order to be effective with "evangelizing conversations," we needed to be able to use our personal stories, because it is much easier to accept a person standing in front of you sharing their story than an abstract set of ideas that call upon you to change the way you normally think and live.

With that in mind, once we started having regular meetings, we saved the last five minutes at the end of each meeting for one person to give a short personal testimony so that we could practice this skill. Some people in the seminary were skeptical about evangelizing through personal testimony because it seemed to them like a technique used by non-Catholics that evoked emotion instead of invoking the truth of the Catholic faith. We developed a talk to explain why personal testimony is important in Catholic evangelization. Pointing out that it has been present from the beginning, we instructed the missionaries-in-training how to give effective personal testimonies.

We looked at the commission that Jesus gave to evangelize, recorded in every one of the Gospel traditions and reflected in the recent teaching of the Church about evangelization from Vatican II forward (and which has since been reaffirmed with Pope Francis' exhortation *Evangelii Gaudium*, The Joy of the Gospel). This led us to the conclusion that every Christian is called to evangelize. Looking at the example of the woman at the well in John 4, we realized that people would come to faith through our witness, just as the Samaritans believed the woman's story about her encounter with Jesus. We read in 1 Peter 3:15 that we should "always be ready to give an explanation to anyone who asks you for a reason for your hope," and this gave us a firm foundation to understand why we should talk about our own experience with Jesus as a way to invite others to grow in their relationship with God.

When you are talking about a personal testimony, you are simply answering the question "Why am I a Catholic disciple of Jesus Christ?" This style of testimony is something that St. Paul uses throughout his epistles; it's an essential biblical form of rhetoric. To lack personal testimony is really to step away from the methodology of Christ and the apostles. What Jesus is actually doing with the parables is telling people their testimonies. When he uses examples of tax collectors and farmers, he's showing them the opportunities they have to know God. St. Paul shares his testimony powerfully in the New Testament—how he "persecuted the church of God beyond measure and tried to destroy it" (Galatians 1:13). In Philippians, his most joyful letter, he warns the community that they should beware of having confidence "in the flesh" and then tells how he was a true son of Israel, a Pharisee, and a persecutor of the church. "[But] whatever gains I had, these I have come to consider a loss because of Christ" (3:4, 7). Paul wants to experience Christ and "the power of his resurrection" (3:10), and so testimony is the constant means he uses of delivering the kerygma.

And that goes back to the importance of the *communio* we experience in contemplation of the Gospels, because you learn how to talk about Jesus and the faith in the same way that they do in the Bible. You talk about it in a way that says, "This is my experience." It's not head knowledge; it's experiential knowledge. Blessed Pope Paul VI wrote, "Modern man listens more willingly to witnesses than to teachers, and if he does listen to teachers, it is because they are witnesses" (*Evangelii Nuntiandi,* 41).

The talks are helpful and important, but it's in that *communio* that the missionaries begin to grow in love for one another, and it's there that they really practice so that their testimony is just something that comes out of them naturally. So what's happening by this fellowship is that we are growing more and more in love for one another and for Jesus. If you have one log and you drench it in lighter fluid, it will burn for a long time; it might even burn all the way down. But if you put on another log, you are going to get a flame. And if you put on another log, it's going to become a real fire. If you pile enough logs on, it's going to be a bonfire, and it's going to be pretty hard to put out. This kind of *communio* and the practice of testimony help us remember how we came to believe, and so we are thinking about doctrines in a personal way. So while it's practice, it's more than that—it's lighting us up; it's fanning the flame of the one log into a bonfire. This is the practical aspect of *communio* in the discipleship process. It's really there that we get formed and get really comfortable talking about Jesus.

How Did You Come to Believe?

Learning to give your testimony in three minutes is crucial because people aren't going to stick around for long, but they will listen to a three-minute testimony. A good personal testimony should include some statement of faith in Jesus Christ as God and man and as Savior of the world—as your Savior. He who saved you is saving you and will save you if you continue to cooperate with his grace, which he freely gives through the sacramental life that he established in the Catholic Church. When you tell someone your testimony, you are answering these questions: "Why are you a Catholic Christian?" "Why do you believe in Jesus Christ?" "Why do you believe and hold to all the teachings of the Catholic faith?"

We looked at Acts 26 and found a great example of personal testimony in the preaching of St. Paul. There are four essential parts of a personal testimony:

1. Life before I knew Jesus Christ (Acts 26:1-11)

In the first stage, you should talk about what kind of person you were socially, spiritually, and emotionally. You should also present a unifying theme to your testimony.

2. How I came to know Jesus Christ (Acts 26:12-18)

In this stage, share what happened to you. Even if your conversion was gradual, your testimony should include some turning point during which you made a decision. If other people played important roles in this transition, you should include that as well. It is important not to overdramatize this moment of conversion.

3. My life in Jesus Christ (Acts 26:19-23)

As a result of the decision you made to cling to Christ and his Church, you should talk about the resulting changes that have happened in your life. You should explain how you are living in relationship with Jesus. As best you can, make sure that you do not use words that will go over the heads of those listening to you. Specific spiritual terms like "vocation," "*lectio divina*," or "dark night of the soul" will likely be unfamiliar to the people you typically meet.

4. The challenge and invitation to the listener (Acts 26:25-29)

You should give your listener an invitation they can take away from the conversation. Finally, invite them to respond to your testimony.

While following this outline, you should still aim at including all the points in three to five minutes. In any given moment of testimony, you should focus on communicating one point (your unifying theme from step one). If you try to do too much with one testimony, you can easily bore your listeners, or even yourself! In order to avoid this, make the testimony *concrete, accessible,* and *simple.*

Some may say, "I have always been Catholic and haven't done anything exciting." Sharing your personal testimony is not about having an exciting story to tell, because you will not be the central focus in a good testimony. A personal testimony relates your personal experience of how Jesus Christ has worked in your life. No one else can tell your story for you, and you don't know how your story will affect the people who listen to it. Whether they see in your experience a powerful similarity to their own life or an arrestingly different way of life that challenges their assumptions, you trust that by speaking about your concrete experience of Christ's saving love, God will touch and call the people to whom he has sent you as a missionary.

The purpose of talking about the concrete ways in which Christ has touched your life is to help other people have an encounter with Jesus. As Pope Benedict XVI said in his encyclical *Deus Caritas Est,* "Being Christian is not the result of an ethical choice or a lofty idea, but the encounter with an event, a person, which gives life a new horizon and a decisive direction" (1). In the second volume of his three-volume work *Jesus of Nazareth,* Pope Benedict wrote, "I . . . hope that I have been granted an insight into the figure of our Lord that can be helpful to all readers who seek to encounter Jesus and to believe in him."[15] We are trying to share our personal encounter with Jesus, our personal testimonies, so that other people can have an encounter with Jesus.

In order to do this, it is important to show your emotions and affections very clearly when talking about Jesus. People can be very solemn, serious, and unemotional when talking about Jesus, especially seminarians. While this is a way to show respect, when you are talking to people who don't already have the reverence and respect for Christ that you do, speaking in this way can tend to shut them out rather than invite them into a relationship with Christ. When people talk about something they really care about, like a football game or a movie, you can see their enjoyment of it in their facial expressions, and their enthusiasm is infectious. We trained missionaries at the Mount to show their emotions and excitement about Christ, the Church, and the faith in the way they speak and through nonverbal communication tools as well.

In the training, we remind the missionaries about the longing that every human person has for happiness. Plato knew it; Aristotle knew it. Augustine found peace and rest with God, and this is exactly how Aquinas starts talking about the Christian response to God—by talking about happiness and showing that only God can make human beings perfectly happy. Through contemplating Christ in the Scriptures, we start to recognize that Jesus was very joyful. This makes sense to us because humanity comes closest to God in his incarnate Person; of all humans, Jesus knew and loved God the Father best because he is God the Son. If we can show that knowing Christ in and through the Church has made us happy, then others start to think about the possibility of choosing that path for themselves.

Once you are familiar with the general pattern of personal testimony, then you can speak about any number of particular ideas or themes as they appear in or relate to your story. Sharing concrete stories of faith is a powerful tool for evangelization because people can see ideas and Catholic teachings "in the flesh," and it makes it easier for them to imagine accepting those teachings for themselves. A hidden benefit of sharing the faith and explaining it through your personal history is that you will also have a powerful encounter with God. Telling other people about God's love for you, and thinking about how you came to accept the teachings of the Church, helps you, the evangelizer, see God's work in your own life and appreciate God's merciful love through your personal history.

Practicing Testimonies

After having taught why and how to give personal testimonies, we practiced giving them for many weeks. We practice testimonies as a response to questions such as "What's the whole deal with Mary?" We try to make every kerygma a testimony (by talking about how the gospel is personal and historical for me) and every testimony a kerygma (by making everything we share about ourselves point to Christ, the Church, and the whole gospel message). This helps the missionaries learn to think on their feet and respond effectively off-the-cuff. They get ready to answer questions we expect to hear: "Why are you a disciple?" "Why do you worship the saints?" Missionaries answer by saying things like "To be honest, I had the same question myself," and then they explain how they came to understand the Church's teaching and embrace it. They've thought through their own story, and the pedagogy that God used for them to come to believe it themselves, and they have become very convincing instruments of the truth because they're real and authentic. They're not just reciting a creed or stating a doctrine. And they're not presuming you know anything about it at all. They learn how to talk about it as though you're ignorant of everything, but in a loving, not a condescending, way. One seminarian named Jacob had an experience like this on a mission trip, which can provide an example of this method.

A person came up to Jacob with his Bible, and they talked for a while. The guy said to Jacob, "I don't understand why you Catholics worship Mary." Jacob answered that we don't worship Mary.

"Really, I thought that's what Catholics did," the guy replied. "Why do you believe in Mary?"

Jacob explained that he grew up in a nondenominational community, so he had to deal with that same question. He learned that the Church had struggled in the first few centuries of its existence to define who Jesus is. It concluded that since Jesus is both man and God, then Mary is not just the mother of Jesus but also the Mother of God and thus deserves to be highly honored. All the saints are venerated because they were truly transformed in Christ and are now in heaven. Because Mary is the Mother of God, we give her special veneration, but we do not worship her; we do not treat her as if she is the Creator instead of a creature. Jacob explained that after he understood the Church's teaching, he still had to make the decision to pray the Rosary and learn the proper way to speak to Mary. As a result of Jacob giving his testimony, this guy learned more about Mary and Catholic beliefs and practices. The guy later talked with a whole group of people about Mary based on what he had learned from Jacob, and at a later point, he even ended up becoming Catholic.

The missionaries have thought through their own stories and looked for ways in which God has taught them and helped them to grow. They then turn around and use the same methods with the people they encounter by sharing their stories of faith. We practice not only what to say and how to make the gospel and the Church concrete through personal testimony, but also how to talk about the faith as if the listener is completely ignorant of the Church, Christianity, or religion and to always speak in a loving way. In the next chapter, we'll describe the techniques and methods we use for having this kind of loving, evangelizing conversation. But before we do so, here are a few examples of personal testimonies, which can show some of the things we've explained in this chapter.

Examples of Testimonies

I was raised Catholic, but I never really heard the gospel proclaimed: that Jesus died for me, that Jesus wanted to have a personal relationship with me, that he is offering himself to me, Body, Blood, Soul, and Divinity, in the Eucharist. Then one day I heard a priest preach about these things and my faith came alive. I came to believe all of this. My prayer changed; it became a real conversation, and my life has changed—yes, slowly—but I look back now four years later, and I am truly not the same person that I was. The love of Jesus Christ has transformed me.

❊ ❊ ❊ ❊ ❊

I have always believed in the teachings of the Church and have faithfully gone to church every Sunday since my baptism as an infant. I have never doubted; I have tried to stay away from serious sin. Of course, I am a bit prideful at times; I was a difficult older brother and sometimes stayed out later than my parents wanted me to. In all of this, however, I know that if it were not for the grace of God given to me in the Eucharist and the sacraments of salvation that he has given to the Catholic Church, I would be the worst sinner of all. None of my success or victory over sin and vice, or anything at all, is sustained by my own efforts. Everything is his gift, and for that I am so grateful. Do I struggle? Of course! But I know and I believe firmly that no matter the struggle, whether sin or tragedy, the only and best way is to bring it all to Jesus, who sustains us in our difficulties.

❈ ❈ ❈ ❈ ❈

For me, the greatest struggle was the moral teachings of the Church. I believed intellectually in the Creed and the basic tenets of the faith, but I did not believe in the teachings of the Church on marriage. "Why is the Church so inconsiderate of peo (3:10) ple's real-life marriage struggles?" I thought. "They need to get with the times and see that people are not robots." But I knew that if I was going to criticize the Church, I needed to ground my stance in real knowledge, truly understanding the moral teaching of the Church from "their" perspective. So I began to study it, and I realized that I didn't understand it properly.

My view was based on the idea that the Church had not really considered the real-life situations of people today—but the Church takes them into greater consideration, more thorough consideration, and more compassionate consideration than any other group out there. My even greater surprise was in coming to learn that the solution, the way that the Church suggests, is superior to that of any other organization, church, community, or philosophical/psychological stance around.

As a result of this more thorough consideration of the Church's teaching and, most of all, a more honest look at the teachings of Jesus Christ in the Gospels, I was converted. As I have considered the faith and all the teachings of the Catholic Church more and more thoroughly, I have come to see and to believe and to be converted more and more on every level. Truly my life is better as a result of pursuing the truth, even if it has meant hard study of the real teachings of the Catholic faith.

❋ ❋ ❋ ❋ ❋

In truth, I cannot say that I can relate to your struggles or opinions with _____. However, I wonder if someone who loves God and also loves you has ever explained it to you. I am no saint; I am no great intellectual; I am just a simple Catholic who believes in Jesus Christ and all that he has handed on to his Church through the apostles. If you would like, I would be happy to try to explain the teaching of the Church for you, but before I do, I must say one thing first. Through the sacraments and in my prayer, I have come to believe and to experience a love that nothing and no one in the world can give. It is the love of Jesus Christ poured out for me in his death. It is a love so beautiful and good that no words can describe it, and as I go deeper and deeper into the mystery of his great love for me, I am convinced that all of his teachings are true, good, and really the only sure way to happiness in this life and the next.

So I must say this from my own experience: God loves you, he's in love with you, and he longs to have a relationship with you—it is for this reason that he died for you on the cross. So on behalf of the Church and the authority given by Jesus Christ, I invite you to receive his great love for you and say yes to the offer of salvation that he holds before you.

❋ ❋ ❋ ❋ ❋

I was raised Catholic, but especially in high school I began to question my faith. At least in my heart and if not in my practice, I really stopped living the faith. I never rejected or denied the faith outright, but I didn't want to think about it or know more about it because I knew that if it were true, I would have to accept everything about it. About that same time, I started working for a place called Rental Works. My boss was just a humble, simple shop owner in a tool rental store, but he had been a youth minister before opening his shop, and he would talk to me about Jesus once in a while

He also hired a cool guy named Josh who was a Christian but kind of a rebel. He had a tattoo across his stomach that said, "Thug for Christ." We hung out, and he would ask me what I thought about religion, and after a few months I said Jesus was probably just a prophet and not God. You don't necessarily have to believe in him to go to heaven, I said; you could be Buddhist or Hindu and you would go to heaven as long as you were a sincere person. When I said this, I remember exactly the intersection where we were stopped at a light. He said, "According to what the Bible says, if I were to pull out into traffic right at this moment and we both died, I would go to heaven, and," he said, pointing to me, "you would go to hell." I kind of smiled and replied, "Hey, man, I thought we were friends." I realized that he didn't say that because he wanted me to go to hell but because he wanted me to go to heaven. It didn't convince me, but I realized that I didn't really know enough about the Bible to reject it; I thought logic was enough for me, and it seemed logical to say that whatever faith you believed in, if you were sincere, you would go to heaven. So I decided at that point that I was going to read the whole Bible and decide for myself who Jesus is.

I graduated from high school and didn't want to go to college right away, and so I traveled around, and I had the Gospels with me and was reading them the whole time. I was traveling with a buddy named Gus, and we ended up in Rome the day after I had read Matthew 16, when Jesus tells Peter, "Upon this rock I will build my church" [verse 18].

We were walking through the city, just going with the flow, and there were thousands of people walking in the same direction. And so we asked a few people what was going on, and we found out that it was Ash Wednesday. And then after following the crowd for some time, we looked up and realized that we were in St. Peter's Square. I looked over the crowd two hundred yards ahead and saw this guy in a white robe with white on his head. "Gus, it's the pope!" I got really excited and jumped over the first fence. I got to the third fence before the Swiss Guard stopped me. I was only thirty yards away from Pope John Paul II. I took his picture, and I realized that there was a pope before him, and before that, all the way back to Peter, this guy in the Gospels, and Peter knew Jesus. And somehow, by the grace of God, at that moment, in St. Peter's Square on Ash Wednesday in the year 2000, the grace of my baptism took effect in my soul through faith. I came to believe that Jesus truly was the Son of God, the Messiah. And I've never looked back since.

CHAPTER 7

Teamwork in Evangelization: Going Out Pairs

Teamwork in evangelization is vital. Intercessory prayer support is the lifeblood of missionary work; it keeps us docile to the Holy Spirit and protects us against spiritual attack. When we organize a mission trip from the Mount, we establish a core team. We discern who feels called to take on the responsibility of leadership and keep our ears open for unexpected inspirations from the Holy Spirit (more on that in this book's conclusion).

Once the core team is chosen, we ask for volunteers to sign up. After sign-ups, the core team prays intensely, taking a lot of time to discern how to group the missionaries into teams. We match missionaries in pairs, then group three pairs together into a team of six, and assign a core team member to each team of six. In our day and age, there are many reasons to send missionaries in pairs, but the one that inspired us the most was the fact that Jesus sent his disciples out two by two, as recorded in Luke 10:1-12.

This passage is important. Jesus "appointed seventy-two others whom he sent ahead of him in pairs to every town and place he intended to visit" (Luke 10:1). This follows chapter 9 of Luke's Gospel, where Jesus chooses the twelve apostles and sends them out—likely two by two—to proclaim the kingdom of God (verses 1-2). Later in that chapter, Jesus predicts his passion and then lays out the conditions of discipleship, which involves taking up the cross (verses 22-25). So discipleship, the proclamation of the gospel, and the love between the disciples go hand in hand. Jesus says, "This is how all will know that you are my disciples, if you have love for one another" (John 13:35). He wants others to see the love that his disciples have in fellowship with one another.

Since we are confident that the Church exists to evangelize, the Lord doesn't want us to just treat this as some program where we can insert anyone into each position. Choosing whom to pair up is one of the most important parts of the mission. The way the men love each other communicates the gospel as powerfully as the words they use. That's why we spent weeks praying about it.

In discerning who would be on each team, and especially in each pair of missionaries, the core team was looking for compatibility and complementarity. Putting an athlete with a more academic-type missionary equips the pair of them to talk to a wide range of different people. It is important that missionaries who are paired together can work together, but they don't have to start out the best of friends.

We trained the missionaries to communicate with each other very frankly so that they could effectively help each other polish up their communication skills and self-presentation. For example, after spending time in training together, missionary pairs might say things to each other like "You do this or that all the time; it doesn't bother me, but it might bother others."

We instruct the missionaries to seek this kind of feedback from each other so that they can identify their blind spots in conversation skills and in their knowledge of the faith. Through this process, even though we paired together guys who might not have a lot in common, they often end up becoming great friends. You can hear this when they come to share about their mission experiences after the fact. By preparing in this way, praying for each other and evangelizing together, missionaries really grow in love for one another. The love that missionaries have for their evangelization partners ends up being a powerful witness to the people they are evangelizing.

The teams (three missionary pairs with a core team member as leader) meet together at least once a week for forty days before they go on mission to practice proclaiming the kerygma and their personal testimonies and to do meditations on Gospel passages. In their teams, the missionaries get really comfortable talking about Jesus. It's basically the practical aspect of *communio* in the wheel of discipleship that we explained in chapter 2. It is in these consistent team meetings that the missionaries get formed and prepared for mission work. The talks we give each week are important, but in the teams the missionaries grow in love for one another, building friendships that are the backbone of the conversational evangelization we do. In their teams, missionaries develop their awareness of the ways that God has worked in their lives and their ability to explain and apply those realizations in personal testimonies that preach the kerygma.

Talking Together with Jesus

One of the consistent activities we do once we arrive at the mission site but before we go out to have evangelizing conversations is small-group meditations on passages from Scripture. We do this throughout the training, but it is important to do it again on the mission site in the days before the main work of the mission begins. It is so easy at that point to get caught up in all the logistical details of preparing for the mission, so it is important to focus our attention on Jesus, on what God is saying to us through the Scriptures at that moment, and on what he wants to do in our lives.

The leader of the team reads the passage out loud, and then the team members simply talk about it. And the first questions we always ask are "What struck your heart? How did God speak to you in this Gospel passage?" From there we just talk together about Jesus.

One of our favorite passages is John 1:35-39. Jesus has been baptized the day before, and he's walking by the same spot; and John stands up and says, "Behold, the Lamb of God, who takes away the sins of the world," and the two disciples with John get up and follow Jesus down the road. And then Jesus turns to the disciples and says, "What do you seek?" and they say, "Where are you staying?" Jesus replies, "Come and see," and they go and stay with him that day. It's a simple passage, but when you sit and talk and think through it with other disciples, it just kind of explodes off the page.

After ten or fifteen minutes, what was once black-and-white from an ancient text becomes living color with surround sound and blue screen and not just an idea. You've actually placed yourself in the passage and you're there with the first disciples of Christ, and you realize that Jesus is guiding the conversation. And you experience Jesus' words: "For where two or three are gathered together in my name, there am I in the midst of them" (Matthew 18:20). And suddenly you hear Jesus speaking to you and to your fellow missionaries, saying, "What do you most desire? What do you most seek?" You're no longer talking to each other, but you're in a conversation with Jesus together as his disciples, discussing the deepest longings of your heart.

The reality that you're sitting there talking together with Jesus makes it a transformative experience. You're really engaging with God, and he's engaging with you through this fellowship of disciples. And then you start to think about your desires in a new way. You start to see how maybe some of your desires are not what they ought to be, and that some are actually from God himself. In the fellowship of your teammates, there are many voices to affirm the good. There's the presence of God with the Scriptures and in the disciples gathered in Jesus' name, and through this, God is tweaking your perspective. You thinking is literally being changed. Like St. Paul wrote in Romans 12:1, "Be transformed by the renewal of your mind." This is happening on a very human level; it's not just this deep spiritual encounter—that would be great—but we also need Jesus to form us in fellowship with others.

Searching for Happiness

What does this have to do with evangelization? What you want to do—the whole goal—is to lead the people you are evangelizing to have an encounter with Christ. And in the deepest part of your personality, you need to have this love and excitement about talking about Jesus. Your affections and emotions need to be very evident to people when you are talking about Jesus.

What people really want is happiness. If you can convince them that what you have will bring them happiness, then they're going to come back again and again. I've asked probably 500 to 800 people if they think Jesus smiled or if they think Jesus was happy, and then they think about it and say hesitantly, "Yes." And then I'll say, "Do you think that Jesus was the happiest person that lived?" And even Christians will say, "I don't know about that." But we are made for happiness; our final end, our *telos*, is happiness. And everything we do in this life is ultimately meant to lead us to perfect happiness, and that is in the contemplation of God in the communion of saints. Jesus is the physical revelation of God.

And so to see Jesus, to encounter Jesus, is meant to be the happiest experience we can have in this life. It is, objectively, but the way Jesus is often talked about is so solemn, uninspired, and lacking in enthusiasm. People don't seem to sense that they are encountering someone that has come to know the living God. But Jesus, a divine Person with a human nature, really was the happiest individual ever to walk the earth. And the more we did these Gospel contemplations together, and the more we came into contact with each other, the more we came to believe, not just in our minds, but through experience, that Jesus always radiated the joy of the Father (see Colossians 1:15). Now, when we think about Jesus, having done these Gospel contemplations so many times, we think that when he smiles, there is no one who can help but smile too.

We see an example of this in St. Philip Neri. He was so joyful that if you were in the same neighborhood as he was, you would suddenly become happy and joyful. You would become free of any kind of navel-gazing despair. And he was just a disciple, a follower of Christ. Jesus has to be able to bring us greater happiness than that. St. Philip Neri was called the second apostle of Rome. Even in his lifetime, he was called "St. Philip." And the way he evangelized Rome was by gathering small groups of disciples together and just talking about Jesus.

Preparing for Rejection

We also do some preparation for rejection. Many Gospel passages talk about Christians experiencing rejection, and Christ's earthly life ended, of course, with his passion and death. Certainly we have all experienced some rejection during the mission trips. Trying to see this with the eyes of faith, we like to look at it as purification more than persecution. According to Jesus' famous teaching in the Beatitudes (Matthew 5:11-12), being insulted, persecuted, and slandered for Jesus' sake is cause for rejoicing! So in rejection you're literally receiving a blessing from someone who might feel hatred toward you. In the passage from Luke 10, Jesus told the seventy-two that some towns would not receive them (verses 10-12). So when they experience rejection, the pairs need to get together and pray with each other and realize, "I've just experienced what Jesus said would happen." This is a powerful way to walk through the passion in solidarity with Christ, to experience the rejection that he experienced. In faith, we know that with Christ, death is followed by resurrection, and so we can rejoice and have hope in the Lord, who can change hearts and bring eternal life out of crucifixion.

In that passage from Luke, when the seventy-two return and share their stories, the Lord "rejoiced in the holy Spirit" (10:21). "Rejoice" does not really convey the emotion here; when it says Jesus rejoiced, it is meant to be extremely emphatic. There are only a few other places in the Gospels where we see Jesus rejoicing. In John 15, he says he loves the disciples as the Father loves him. He urges them to "remain in his love," and adds, "I have told you this so that my joy may be in you and your joy may be complete" (verses 10-11). So Jesus rejoices in the Holy Spirit because his disciples have experienced being loved by God and loving each other, thus revealing to others that they are disciples of Christ.

"Stop, Drop, and Roll"

We developed a rule called "Stop, Drop, and Roll" that is a form of accountability between evangelizing partners while they are in the middle of an evangelizing conversation. We introduce this tool once we are on-site at the mission and once the partners have had a chance to get to know each other pretty well. The partners establish some kind of signal for when one partner is getting off track in a conversation. The wingman says, "Where are we going with this?" or uses a physical signal like tapping his nose or arm. Then the other person reels himself in, using lines like "I don't want to take up your whole day" or "We're kind of talking a lot here." If the person you are trying to evangelize declines the escape, then the partner who stepped in has shown his concern but has also set up the conversation to go to a deeper level. On the other hand, it is really important for evangelizing partners to trust each other; sometimes when one missionary is really excited about sharing the gospel, it can be easy for him to miss important communication signals from the person he wants to evangelize, and thus he can inadvertently turn off that person to the gospel in different ways without knowing it. I hope a few of the stories that follow illustrate how we use "Stop, Drop, and Roll" and how effective this tool can be.

On one mission trip, a first-year seminarian named Jeremy and a deacon named Sam were paired together. These guys really complemented each other well because Jeremy is the most pleasant guy you can imagine, but he was just getting started in his studies, and so, by his own admission, he didn't know much theology. Sam was a transitional deacon who had been in business before seminary, had studied sales, and was a good salesman, but he was a little more introverted than Jeremy. Both guys loved sports. They decided together that this would be their starting point in conversations with people, especially the sports teams at the school they were visiting.

It was Sam's first trip and Jeremy's second, but Jeremy still felt uncomfortable because he was just beginning his studies. They had decided that they would take turns choosing a person to speak with and initiating the conversation. So they were inside a building on campus, and it was Jeremy's turn to pick someone to approach. There were all these open rooms where they could find someone to talk to, but there was also a room in this building for resting; it was dark, and there were college kids leaning against beanbags. Most of the students there were taking naps. And Jeremy looked in, back to the darkest part of the room, at the back, and he saw a guy on his phone, half asleep, with his head down. And Jeremy said, "That guy. Let's go talk to that guy." Sam said, "No, that's a terrible idea, but okay, you lead the way."

They walked into the nap room, and they were literally walking over students in the dark to get to the back of the room. Jeremy started up a conversation with this guy, who was probably feeling that this was a little weird that these guys were trying to talk to him. Jeremy introduced himself and asked what his name was. Sam was standing back but then jumped into the conversation.

"Wait a second. What did you say your name is?" After hearing the answer, Sam asked, "What kind of name is that?"

"It's Turkish, actually," came the reply.

"Are both your parents Turkish?" Sam asked. They were.

"Were you born in the US or in Turkey?"

"I was born in Turkey, but my dad had lived in the US before he went back to Turkey and married my mom. And then they moved back here to Maryland with me and my brothers."

"Where in Maryland?" The guy named the town.

Sam said, "That's funny. That's where I'm from. Did you stay with a family or did you have your own house?" The guy said that they stayed with a family in Maryland. Sam asked, "Was their last name 'Wilson'?"

"Yes," the guy said with a curious look.

Sam said with a smile on his face, "I'm Sam Wilson. I haven't seen you since you were four years old."

And the guy said, "Holy Smokes!"

That night there was a big Catholic ministry event on campus, and the guy, who was a nominal Muslim, couldn't come because he had a class. He and Sam ended up talking about Jesus and Christianity. He didn't know anything about Christianity and had never been told about Jesus. Sam invited him back to his family's house to meet them again. Since then, Sam has talked to him at different points and is slowly working on helping him to have a relationship with Jesus Christ.

Jeremy and Sam worked out a system for how they were going to coordinate and help each other. They were both scared. But Jeremy is bolder and also more innocent by nature. He can walk into a situation, like that resting room, which would be creepy for Sam on his own. But Jeremy can just start up conversations in all kinds of circumstances. Sam was stretched in that moment, and he had to choose to love Jeremy in that situation. By loving Jeremy and trusting him, there was an opportunity for this guy, who had lived in Sam's house as a boy, to encounter Christ.

Another seminarian at the time, Thomas Gallagher, was paired up with a seminarian named Roberto from Columbia when we were on a mission at Ball State University in Indiana. They were in the library, and Roberto chose to go and talk to one of the students.

The guy was a nominal Catholic, and Thomas noticed that every time this guy was speaking in response to him, he was being resistant. Thomas was really feeling bold that day and he said, very directly, "Religion aside, you have an obstinate spirit. You're never going to be able to receive the truth in any form until you work on your resistance to listening." And the guy really heard these words. Thomas continued, "If you want, I can go on. But I can't do anything for you unless you want to listen." The guy said, "Okay, talk." Thomas started talking about the Eucharist and the love of God, and the guy wanted him to go on, and he was actually getting into it.

Then Roberto chimed in and said, "Where are we going with this?" (Thomas invented the phrase "Where are we going with this?") Thomas felt like Roberto was off point, but he submitted to him. So Thomas looked at Roberto and said, "Please, you speak." Roberto asked the guy, "Are you getting this? Is this helpful, because we don't want to be overbearing." The guy said, "No, this is actually great. No one has ever told me this straight. This is very helpful." Thomas and Roberto loved each other in that moment and were also able to love another person better because there were two of them. With evangelization in pairs, you can build off the points each missionary is making: stopping once in a while, asking how the person is doing, helps to keep any one of the missionaries from becoming overbearing and helps move the conversations along. Evangelization happens in community. You feed off of each other; you grow from each other and can build off each other's arguments. But you also have to hold back from speaking as well. You really have to develop that friendship beforehand so that you know how each other communicates and can help each other out.

On our first mission trip, at the end of the first day, the campus chaplain brought in dinner for all of us, which we did not expect. We were sitting around eating our food, and guys started sharing stories about their conversations and experiences that day. Sharing stories from our evangelizing experiences has become an integral part of the mission trips. It gives the missionaries a taste of apostolic zeal for souls and an experience of God's joy. Just as the seventy-two disciples returned rejoicing from the mission that Jesus had sent them on (Luke 10:17), so we share our experiences of the mission. When we share our stories about the evangelization we do, we have a parallel experience of rejoicing in the Spirit. This helps us see the fruit of the work we are doing as we become attentive to the Spirit's promptings and cooperate with his action to save souls and build up the kingdom of God.

CHAPTER 8

"Closing the Deal": Inviting People into Deeper Faith

After the training the missionaries receive about how to start evangelizing conversations and keep them going, we also give them tools for "closing the deal" by inviting the people they talk with on mission into a deeper relationship with Christ in the Church. We use the five "thresholds of conversion" as a starting point:

1. Initial trust
2. Spiritual curiosity
3. Spiritual openness
4. Spiritual seeking
5. Intentional discipleship[16]

We combine this list with other systems in Church tradition, such as St. Teresa of Avila's seven mansions in her *Interior Castle*, and conclude by recognizing that in an individual person's faith journey, there are perhaps more stages than these systems record. What is important is being attentive to what God wants to do through us at this point.

Although a missionary might not have the blessing of seeing someone embrace intentional discipleship, our goal is to help people progress along the path of discipleship. After engaging them in an evangelizing conversation, they might only move to "initial trust" in us, but in the Lord's plan for this person's journey, maybe that is the part we are called to play on that given day. We need to accept whatever progress we see toward mature faith as what it is: a gift from God for them and for us.

In any evangelizing conversation, the goal of presenting the kerygma through your personal testimony is to prepare the listener to accept God's love for them and, believing in it, to come into deeper union with the Lord through the sacraments and the body of Christ, his Church. In every evangelistic conversation, the missionary should include an invitation to pursue faith further. Usually, in our experience, this happens at the end of the conversation. It is important, however, for the missionary to be attentive to the promptings of the Spirit in case the person is moving to this point in the midst of their conversation.

Different missionaries at the Mount use different introductory lines, such as "I have just one quick thing to tell you . . . " or "Has anyone ever shown you what Jesus said about having a relationship with him?" Clearly, there are many ways to queue up to the final pitch. We follow up this one-line introduction by referring to, or perhaps reciting, some parts of compact Scripture texts that talk about Christian discipleship. John 14:15-23 and 1 John 4:9–5:3 are two that we've used in training missionaries before. Using these texts, we present some of the essentials of Christian discipleship:

1. Acceptance in faith
2. Sacraments of Initiation

3. Acceptance of and obedience to Jesus' commandments

4. A life of prayer

For the first step, we focus on the Scriptures in their entirety and the Creed as an expression of the faith handed on from the apostles. When we talk about the Sacraments of Initiation (Baptism, Confirmation, and Eucharist), we focus on them as the signs of the new and everlasting covenant established in Christ—that is, the permanent and regular doorway through which we are invited by Christ and the Church to participate in God's life of love.

The passages from John's Gospel and the First Letter of John emphasize the importance of following God's commandments as a sign and proof of love for God. This means that having a relationship puts demands on our behavior and can challenge us to change the way we live. It is interesting to point out to people that a friendship of any kind beyond the surface level sets limits for our actions, and being friends with God is no exception! Finally, we speak about the life of prayer as the time we spend communicating with God, taking time to talk to him and also, more important, listening to his words to us.

At this point, we invite people to pray right then and there to begin a relationship with Jesus or to deepen it if they have already begun that relationship. All the missionaries have copies of a commitment prayer (of which there are many, of course). This is the one we hand out:

Jesus, come into my life. Reveal yourself to me. Free me from my sins and lead me to the truth. Reveal to me your mercy in the power of your resurrection. Lord Jesus Christ, prove to me your love and lead me to everlasting life. Amen.

After praying this prayer together, we have the people we are evangelizing read this text on the spot as a follow-up to the commitment prayer:

This prayer should be the beginning of an ongoing living relationship with Jesus Christ, most easily and perfectly lived out in his Church through the grace of the sacraments. This is the purpose of the Catholic Campus Ministry, and their doors are always open.

The last part of our evangelizing conversations is a personal appeal from the missionary to the person. Missionaries are highly encouraged to look the listener in the face when they deliver this final message and not read it from a card. This should be a personal message, expressed with full respect and the utmost love. If you have to look at a paper and read the words, the invitation comes off as a halfhearted formula, which undermines all the work of loving them through the conversation. We started making this invitation in a particular way, including the many important points that we want to communicate clearly. Now it has become a commonly used tool. It's been used before in this book but is worth repeating:

God loves you; he's in love with you, and he longs to have a relationship with you. So on behalf of the Church that Jesus founded, I invite you to come and learn about this God who loves you so much.

We have seen this invitation act as a powerful moment of conversion for countless people. If there is no time at the end of a conversation to follow all the steps of the "closing the deal" training, we encourage missionaries to make sure that they at least deliver this one message above.

The last step of our evangelizing conversations is to give people materials to look at later. These include a Bible (which we raised money to buy and provide); a pamphlet on Catholic teachings (we've used the *Pillar of Fire, Pillar of Truth* pamphlets,[17] but there are many good ones out there); information about the local campus ministry or parish information so that after talking with us, they can have some follow-up with Catholic networks on the ground; and the Facebook page for the seminary so that they can be in touch with us if they'd like to do so. The whole process of "closing the deal" is a pivotal moment for the many people we've talked to on our mission trips, and so we focus on this in the training. We want to make sure that the missionaries practice it enough so that they feel comfortable moving through the steps of inviting people deeper into faith.

CHAPTER 9

The Upper Room:
Immediate Preparation for Mission

As the time approached for our first mission trip, we asked Dr. Love to come and speak to us. He suggested that we ask the Holy Spirit to do whatever he wanted to do on the mission trip. The Holy Spirit is both faithfully consistent and marvelously unpredictable, he told us. God always draws people into a deeper relationship with himself out of his unfathomable love for each one of us. The ways in which he manifests his love for us, and the concrete gifts he gives, are amazingly varied. Sometimes it appears as though "nothing is happening," but you later find out that God has worked powerfully in someone's life. Other times you get to see the glorious fruit of your service to the Lord right away. Dr. Love told the guys he didn't know what was going to happen on the mission trip and that trusting the Holy Spirit would be a wild ride. Even so, he said, we should pray for the Holy Spirit to do whatever he wanted and trust that as the "mover of hearts," he would give whatever the students at George Mason and we, as missionaries, needed.

So for forty days before the mission trip, we were praying daily before the Eucharist in adoration with the Scriptures. From the beginning, we chose Mary, Star of the New Evangelization, as our special patroness. After hearing Dr. Love's advice, we decided to pray a novena to her for nine days before we went to the campus, asking for an outpouring of the Holy Spirit upon us. What we were basically doing for those nine days was imitating the disciples in the upper room before Pentecost, begging the Holy Spirit to come and trusting that he would come and give us power to be good witnesses to Christ, the Church, and the Catholic faith. Before a trip, most of the guys, even on their third or fourth mission, are starting to feel scared. It's a healthy fear, I think, a realistic fear. They are going to the campus and starting up conversations with people they don't know. They are invading their "space." These are people who don't know them and probably already don't like them because, as seminarians, they know the men are Catholic. That's one of the reasons the novena is so important.

For the first trip, we arrived at George Mason University a couple of days before we planned to go out so that we could get situated in our accommodations and oriented to the layout of the campus. We walked around praying the Rosary and claiming the campus for Christ, but Thomas Gallagher and I knew that we needed some pivotal moment of empowerment to calm our fears and entrust everything to the Lord. My friend Rami, who came with us on the first trip and is now with the Franciscan Friars of the Renewal in New York, found an old litany to the Holy Spirit online, and we downloaded it and adapted it for the prayer service we were inspired to have on the night before we finally went out across campus.

We asked the missionaries to split into two groups, one on each side of the chapel where we had gathered. We divided the litany of the Holy Spirit in half so that the two groups of missionaries could alternate the "call" and the "answer" throughout the litany. We began with some songs calling on the Holy Spirit to come, including Latin chants like *Veni Sancte Spiritus* ("Come, Holy Spirit"). Then we prayed the litany. One side chanted various prayers, such as "Come in your power, Holy Spirit," "Come with your fire, Holy Spirit," "Come with your love, Holy Spirit," while the other side repeated the same response, "Come, Holy Spirit." After a while, we switched roles, so that each side of the chapel eventually prayed both parts of the litany.

After a series of invocations like that, we read a Scripture passage about the Holy Spirit and his actions in salvation history. We read John 14, where Jesus tells his disciples that he must go so that the Spirit can come. We read Acts 1, where Jesus tells the apostles to go to Jerusalem and wait for the descent of the Spirit, and the story of Pentecost in Acts 2. We read the story of creation in Genesis 1, where the Spirit hovers over the waters, as well as other Old Testament texts in which people receive the Spirit of the Lord. After reading one passage, we would return to the litany, asking the Holy Spirit to come down upon us.

We continued with this pattern of prayer for one hour, then two, and then we kept going. We were getting tired, but everyone knew that the Holy Spirit was with us like a thick smoke in the chapel. One of the last Scripture passages we read was John 15:1-17, where Jesus explains that he is the vine and we are the branches; apart from him we can do nothing. We read this text slowly, and it helped us meditate on the fact that the evangelization we planned to do was God's work, and that we needed his love, his strength, and his words to reach people's hearts and help them turn to God.

After almost three hours of prayer, we stopped because we knew that we had been blessed and prepared by the Holy Spirit for the work we had come to do. Even though it was late and we'd been there such a long time, the missionaries were remarkably joyful at the end, which is a great sign of the presence of the Spirit. That first time we prayed this way was so powerful; it remains one of the most powerful experiences of my mature Catholic faith life. Obviously, after this experience, we prayed this way for the outpouring of the Holy Spirit on every mission trip the night before we started evangelizing.

When we woke up the next day, we went back to the chapel and prayed for an hour in front of the Blessed Sacrament. We meditated on 1 John 1:1-9, which talks about sharing with others the fellowship we have with Christ, which brings joy and conversion. We had Mass, said a prayer asking for Mary's intercession, and handed out small New Testaments and pamphlets. With a message reassuring the missionaries that they were being sent out by the Holy Spirit, we fanned out across campus to assigned high-traffic locations.

The Holy Spirit was palpable all around us. The presence of God and the joy, love, and peace we experienced then were indescribable. You could lean against the Holy Spirit like you could lean against a brick wall. It was like walking on a cloud of the Holy Spirit. People were smiling at us, and they seemed disposed to us. One student came up to me and told me that he was a photography major who had a project to take portraits of happy people, and he wanted to take my picture for the project. I'm not a very smiley person, but this guy, who had no idea what we were about, recognized the joy that we had. One missionary said to me, "I am certain that these people are going to be open to us. I just feel certain that God is going to use us to communicate to souls today." At certain points I had to calm myself down. I was walking around like a wild man talking about Jesus. This was the beginning of the mission trips from the Mount that have occurred every semester since then.

A Culture of Evangelization

The last topic that Fr. Thomas asked me (John Love) to speak about in the meetings just before the first mission trip was some answer to the question "How should we pray in preparation for missionary work?" I prayed about what I would tell the guys, and among other things, I was reminded of a wonderful, miraculous mission trip I took to Mexico in 2000, the Year of the Great Jubilee.

I told them about the fantastic time we had on that trip building houses, visiting the sick, praying with people, including a man possessed by demons, and sharing our testimonies of faith. On that trip with poor people in the northern deserts near Monterrey and Saltillo, we experienced at least one miracle a day, including one gift I've only seen once in my life.

When we traveled to the outlying villages, we would drive to the chapel and then walk around inviting people to prayer (or Mass if the chaplain was with our small group) and talk with them as best we could. One family was very worried because an aunt in the family had been lying on the ground for three days without moving. The family members asked the missionaries to come and pray for her, and so, although they were not sure what our prayers might do, a few missionaries walked to the place where the woman was.

The small one-room dwelling had a tattered sheet for a door, and the floor was only hard-packed dirt. There were a few tools for cooking, some blankets, and other rudiments of subsistence living. By all evidence of the senses, the woman who lay on the floor seemed to be dead—no movement, no sound, no breathing. Nevertheless, inspired by the faith of the family who believed in the power of prayer, the missionaries prayed as they had been asked. After a short while, the woman sat straight up and immediately began to prepare food for the guests! When I told this part of the story to the men, some eyebrows rose, and a few of them sat up straight in their chairs. But what I said next made some mouths hang open.

The most amazing thing to me about this story was that for ten years, I had almost completely forgotten about it. It's hard to imagine that you could forget the time when somebody was raised from the dead, but the most vivid memories that have stuck with me from the mission work, retreats, and other spiritual activities I've done are the conversions I've been privileged to witness and somehow assist in. Judging from their expressions and posture, this message struck a chord with the guys about to go on the first mission trip we had organized in recent years. After that first trip, the missionaries had tasted for themselves the joy of conversion, and zeal for evangelizing work spread throughout the seminary like fire.

There are many ways to evangelize and participate in the New Evangelization. Pope Francis has issued two different encyclicals—*Lumen Fidei* and *Evangelii Gaudium*—that speak about the New Evangelization, showing that, if anything, the energy and attention of the Church are more focused on this task than it has been since Vatican II. We hope that the information and stories we have shared in this book inspire those who read it to discern the ways in which they can deepen their own Christian discipleship and teach others to do the same. We hope that the description of our methods and experiences in training missionaries for conversational evangelization will be helpful to those who would like to do something like this in their own family, parish, workplace, seminary, or diocese. Over the past few years, these mission trips and the training that goes with them have certainly had a great impact on the culture and formation at the Mount.

From interest in conversational and door-to-door evangelization at the Mount, a student club was formed, with assistance and increasing support from the faculty and administration of the seminary. But it did not remain just a "club," a niche market for those so inclined. Several people took concrete steps to transform the New Evangelization Club, which ran mission trips, into an integral component of the formation offered to future priests at Mount St. Mary's Seminary.

Changing Attitudes

The initial reaction of some seminarians and staff members at the Mount to the New Evangelization Club and its mission trips was actually hostile. From what they saw (which was not always the full extent of the training and experience of the missionaries), they thought that the gospel was being watered down or presented in only partial form and that the methods employed were irrational gimmicks that did not reveal the full splendor of the Catholic faith and tradition. Fr. Thomas strategically sought out seminarians that were well respected by their peers, like one of his classmates with a near-perfect grade point average, and convinced them to do one mission trip. When these guys had amazing experiences of God's work in and through the training program and the actual mission, then the mission trips gained considerable credibility in the wider seminary community. The Holy Spirit also did some of his recruiting for the mission trips, which, in the case of Steve Duquaine, had far-reaching effects on the culture of the mission trips and the seminary itself. We talked to Steve in preparing to write this book and got his perspective on this series of events.

Steve wasn't interested in "doing evangelization" with the New Evangelization Club. He thought of it as "just another FOCUS group"—former missionaries from FOCUS trying to "relive the glory days" of their preseminary lives. Steve couldn't see at that point how the methods and activities of the club connected with the preparation for priesthood that is intended to be delivered in the seminary. With these perceptions and attitudes, and demonstrating his mature docility to the Spirit, Steve discerned in his personal prayer that God was calling him to go on a mission trip with the club.

He said that he dragged his feet during every step of the training and was at least internally critical—the focus on discipleship and a "personal relationship with Jesus" seemed "watered down to him." Steve didn't understand why the men were instructed to say some things and not say other things. Then he actually went on the mission. He was paired with a seminarian that he knew from some ministry they were doing together with the university tennis team at the Mount. Steve said that his first trip was a great experience, and that in the conversations he and his partner had during the mission, he saw the reasons why the training was done. After the trip was over, Steve thought to himself, "Been there, done that." He would give a good report to others but thought he was finished with this evangelizing activity. It was at that point that Fr. Thomas asked Steve to lead the next mission trip.

Although there was a lot of enthusiasm for the trips and great results, Fr. Thomas had discerned with other leaders in the club that the group needed more long-term direction and better organization. As Thomas Gallagher put it, drawing on his experience with the Marines, the group had "a lot of thrust but not enough vector." Steve had gotten a degree in engineering from Purdue before coming to the Mount and is really good at organization. Some of the leaders were worried that increasing the level of organization and systematizing the training more would suck out the organic and Spirit-driven life that made the club really attractive to many. Although the invitation to lead the group was totally unexpected, through prayerful discernment Steve accepted it.

Steve collected, collated, and organized notes for talks and training methods. He made outlines and to-do lists and defined certain jobs for the missionary trips. Organization brought change, but it also gave life to the endeavor by removing the stress of a last-minute, "whack-a-mole" approach to logistical details. The organization and systematization also captured the inspirations and refinements that made the club life-giving and effective so that these could be preserved and passed on even when people like seminarian Thomas Cavanaugh had graduated and become hyper-busy Fr. Thomas Cavanaugh, with a mile-long list of pastoral responsibilities and a constant stream of people seeking care and priestly help. In addition to these contributions, Steve also helped chart the way from a New Evangelization Club at the Mount to a culture of evangelization for the Mount.

More than a Club

Steve thought a lot about the label "club." A club is self-contained and somehow exclusive of nonmembers (you are in or out of a club). Applying this label to those who were interested in participating in the mission trips limited the perception of "evangelizing activity" at the Mount. Steve suggested that the person in charge of the logistical details for the mission trips be called the "New Evangelization mission coordinator," and the person responsible for the spiritual leadership of the training program be called the "discipleship coordinator." He took other steps as well to help transform the culture of the Mount.

After each mission trip, instead of only sharing stories about the mission among those who had made the trip, these "glory story" sessions were opened up to the whole Mount community. This was done to demythologize the mission trips and get more people excited about the fantastic results we were seeing from these missions.

Steve spoke with other groups at the Mount, such as the local chapters of the Legion of Mary, the Militia of the Immaculata, and the Knights of Columbus. He talked with them about using the language of "evangelization" to describe the work they do to spread the gospel and serve the poor. This went so well that the Legion of Mary at the Mount sponsored a parish-based mission trip one fall break, including door-to-door evangelization, and training sessions offered by core team members of the mission trips. Since this fruitful experience, the Mount's Legion of Mary chapter has made at least one door-to-door parish mission trip every semester.

Some seminarians were so excited about the training they got in preparation for the mission trips that they wanted to keep their weekly "team" meetings going. They were hungry for "contemplating the face of Christ" and developing their life of discipleship even when they were not actively preparing for a particular mission. Thus, the mission trips spun off to form the discipleship groups, which aimed at exactly these goals. One of the vice rectors, Fr. Brian Doerr, was excited to help steer this group, along with several of the student core team members from the trips.

Year after year, as more seminarians had been on at least one mission trip, it gradually got to the point where more than half of the seminarians had experienced one, and almost all really liked it. Then we reached the tipping point: as a new class of seminarians arrived at the Mount in the fall of 2013, among the men in the house, it was just normal and expected that every seminarian would go on at least one mission trip. Almost all of the deacon class has been on at least one trip, and several of them have held leadership roles at various times. The administration threw its weight into the mix and established a new requirement that every man participate in at least one mission trip as part of the formation offered at this seminary. This requirement coincides with the sentiment of the men preparing to be priests at this venerable and vibrant seminary: evangelization is important. It is integrally connected to the life of Christian discipleship, and every priest in the twenty-first century formed at the Mount should have training and experience inviting people to deepen their relationship with the Triune God by engaging in the holistic life of faith offered to everyone in the Catholic Church.

We hope that you learn much from the tools and stories we have shared in this book. But above all, we hope that you will share in our joy. We hope that you too wish to go out and share the joy of knowing Christ. It will change your life! You will come to know the joy of sharing in Jesus' mission in a way that so many Catholics do not. You will come to experience the delight of your deepest identity as a Catholic: evangelization! It's no coincidence that Pope Francis' apostolic exhortation is called *Evangelii Gaudium*, The Joy of the Gospel. St. John Paul II wanted to get this message to the world as well when he constantly reminded us, quoting Vatican II, that "Man can fully discover his true self only in a sincere giving of himself" (*Gaudium et Spes*, 24). John Paul's other most quoted line from Vatican II tells us where to find our example of self-giving: "Christ . . . reveals man fully to himself" (22).

At the closing of this book, we want to encourage everyone to engage their faith more deeply and call upon the Holy Spirit to inspire them for the work he has for them to do. Every time we pray the Our Father, we ask that his kingdom come and that his will be done on earth as it is in heaven. We pray now that the Spirit of Jesus will come into our hearts and lead us to do the will of the Father, for the glory of God and the salvation of souls! Amen.

Notes

1. From a letter by St. Clare of Assisi to Blessed Agnes of Prague, used in the Roman Office of Readings for the Feast of St. Clare on August 11.

2. Pope Benedict, Inaugural Homily, April 24, 2005. Accessed at https://w2.vatican.va/content/benedict-xvi/en/homilies/2005/documents/hf_ben-xvi_hom_20050424_inizio-pontificato.html.

3. Fr. Bret A. Brannen, *To Save a Thousand Souls: A Guide to Discerning a Vocation to the Priesthood* (Valdosta, GA: Vianney Vocations, 2010).

4. Kendra Creasy Dean, *Almost Christian: What the Faith of Our Teenagers Is Telling the American Church* (New York: Oxford University Press, 2010).

5. Sherry Weddell, *Forming Intentional Disciples: The Path to Knowing and Following Jesus* (Huntington, IN: Our Sunday Visitor, 2012), 9–70.

6. Ibid., 60.

7. Matthew Kelly, *The Four Signs of a Dynamic Catholic* (Cincinnati, OH: Beacon Publishing, 2012).

8. Stephen J. Rossetti, *Why Priests Are Happy: A Study of the Psychological and Spiritual Health of Priests* (Notre Dame, IN: Ave Maria Press, 2011).

9. Erasmo Leiva-Merikakis, *The Way of the Disciple* (San Francisco: Ignatius Press, 2003), 36.

10. Joseph Cardinal Ratzinger, "The New Evangelization: Building a Civilization of Love." Address to Catechists and Religion Teachers. Jubilee of Catechists, December 12, 2000. Accessed at www.ewtn.com/new_evangelization/Ratzinger.htm.

11. *The Spiritual Exercises of St. Ignatius: Based on Studies in the Language of the Autograph*, trans. Louis J. Puhl, SJ (Chicago: Loyola University Press), 1968, 35.

12. Raoul Plus, SJ, *Radiating Christ: An Appeal to Roman Catholics* (Oak Lawn, IL: CMJ Marian Publishers, 1998).

13. Dale Carnegie, *How to Win Friends and Influence People* (New York: Simon and Schuster, 1964).

14. Francis de Sales, *Introduction to the Devout Life*, SFS Publications and the Indian Institute of Spirituality, chapter 1. Accessed at http://www.philothea.de/devout-english.html.

15. Benedict XVI (Joseph Ratzinger), *Jesus of Nazareth, Part Two, Holy Week: From the Entrance into Jerusalem to the Resurrection* (San Francisco: Ignatius Press, 2011), p. xvii.

16. Sherry Weddell, *Forming Intentional Disciples*, 129–130.

17. The *Pillar of Fire, Pillar of Truth* pamphlet is published by Catholic Answers and is available at http://www.catholic.com/documents/pillar-of-fire-pillar-of-truth.